Cambridge Elements

Elements in International Relations
edited by
Jon C. W. Pevehouse
University of Wisconsin–Madison
Tanja A. Börzel
Freie Universität Berlin
Edward D. Mansfield
University of Pennsylvania
Associate Editors – International Political Economy
Edward D. Mansfield
University of Pennsylvania
Stefanie Walter
University of Zurich

IMF LENDING: PARTISANSHIP, PUNISHMENT, AND PROTEST

M. Rodwan Abouharb
University College London

Bernhard Reinsberg
University of Glasgow

Shaftesbury Road, Cambridge CB2 8EA, United Kingdom

One Liberty Plaza, 20th Floor, New York, NY 10006, USA

477 Williamstown Road, Port Melbourne, VIC 3207, Australia

314–321, 3rd Floor, Plot 3, Splendor Forum, Jasola District Centre, New Delhi – 110025, India

103 Penang Road, #05–06/07, Visioncrest Commercial, Singapore 238467

Cambridge University Press is part of Cambridge University Press & Assessment, a department of the University of Cambridge.

We share the University's mission to contribute to society through the pursuit of education, learning and research at the highest international levels of excellence.

www.cambridge.org
Information on this title: www.cambridge.org/9781009451154

DOI: 10.1017/9781009451116

© M. Rodwan Abouharb and Bernhard Reinsberg 2023

This work is in copyright. It is subject to statutory exceptions and to the provisions of relevant licensing agreements; with the exception of the Creative Commons version the link for which is provided below, no reproduction of any part of this work may take place without the written permission of Cambridge University Press.

An online version of this work is published at doi.org/10.1017/9781009451116 under a Creative Commons Open Access license CC-BY-NC 4.0 which permits re-use, distribution and reproduction in any medium for non-commercial purposes providing appropriate credit to the original work is given. You may not distribute derivative works without permission. To view a copy of this license, visit https://creativecommons.org/licenses/by-nc/4.0/

All versions of this work may contain content reproduced under license from third parties. Permission to reproduce this third-party content must be obtained from these third-parties directly.

When citing this work, please include a reference to the DOI 10.1017/9781009451116

First published 2023

A catalogue record for this publication is available from the British Library

ISBN 978-1-009-45115-4 Hardback
ISBN 978-1-009-45116-1 Paperback
ISSN 2515-706X (online)
ISSN 2515-7302 (print)

The Appendices for this Element can be found here: www.cambridge.org/Abouharb-Reinsberg
Replication Data can also be found here: www.cambridge.org/Abouharb-Reinsberg-Replication-Data

Cambridge University Press & Assessment has no responsibility for the persistence or accuracy of URLs for external or third-party internet websites referred to in this publication and does not guarantee that any content on such websites is, or will remain, accurate or appropriate.

IMF Lending: Partisanship, Punishment, and Protest

Elements in International Relations

DOI: 10.1017/9781009451116
First published online: November 2023

M. Rodwan Abouharb
University College London

Bernhard Reinsberg
University of Glasgow

Author for correspondence: M. Rodwan Abouharb, m.abouharb@ucl.ac.uk

Abstract: This Element argues that governments allocate adjustment burdens strategically to protect their supporters, imposing adjustment costs upon the supporters of their opponents, who then protest in response. Using large-*N* micro-level survey data from three world regions and a global survey, it discusses the local political economy of International Monetary Fund (IMF) lending. It finds that opposition supporters in countries under IMF structural adjustment programs (SAP) are more likely to report that the IMF SAP increased economic hardships than government supporters and countries without IMF exposure. In addition, it finds that partisan gaps in IMF SAP evaluations widen in IMF program countries with an above-median number of conditions, suggesting that opposition supporters face heavier adjustment burdens, and that opposition supporters who think SAPs made their lives worse are more likely to protest. This title is also available as Open Access on Cambridge Core.

Keywords: International Monetary Fund, structural adjustment, distributional politics, protest, survey analysis

© M. Rodwan Abouharb and Bernhard Reinsberg 2023

ISBNs: 9781009451154 (HB), 9781009451161 (PB), 9781009451116 (OC)
ISSNs: 2515-706X (online), 2515-7302 (print)

Contents

1	Introduction	1
2	Theoretical Framework	8
3	Data	19
4	How IMF Programs Affect Distributive Politics	37
5	How Distributive Politics under IMF Programs Affect Protest	68
6	Discussion and Conclusion	98
	References	102

IMF Lending: Partisanship, Punishment, and Protest

1 Introduction

The election year of 2000 in Ghana and 2002 in Kenya saw incumbents President Jerry Rawlings's National Democratic Congress (NDC) and President Daniel arap Moi's Kenya African National Union (KANU) lose to their opposition rivals. While the presidents and their entourages left their palaces, both countries continued with adjustment programs under the International Monetary Fund (IMF).[1] In Ghana, John Agyekum Kufuor, leader of the New Patriotic Party (NPP), moved in, while in Kenya Mwai Kibaki led the National Rainbow Coalition (NARC) into power. Despite the continuity of programs, we see distinct changes between administrations in how they implemented their agreements with the IMF. There is evidence that all administrations, old and new, engaged in distributional politics to cushion their supporters from the burdens of the programs while lumping the costs on to those who supported the opposition. When these governments changed, so too did those who benefited and those who were burdened by these programs. We illustrate our arguments with examples from the cases here.

Ghana was lauded as an IMF darling for its willingness to implement a range of fiscal and monetary conditions. Nevertheless, President Rawlings was sensitive to retaining enough support to keep power, despite coming to the office through a coup (Akonor 2013). He sought to placate domestic opposition and public unrest to the reforms, primarily through the Program of Action to Mitigate the Social Costs of Adjustment (PAMSCAD), launched in 1987 to address the negative socio-economic consequences of IMF agreements beginning in 1983 (Reddy 1998). PAMSCAD was politicized in its design and execution. It prioritized high-visibility projects across the country, rather than just need as a criterion (Gayi 1991). The program aimed to shore up support for the economic recovery program as well as the government, and to improve support for the regime by targeting rural areas in the north of the country (Gayi 1991). Rawlings gave large pay rises to the public sector including civil servants and promoted rural development projects including electrification (Akonor 2013). In contrast to this broad sectoral approach, the Kufuor administration, with its narrower and more concentrated support base, implemented the agreements with the IMF differently. It undertook reforms to promote the indigenous business sector, which Rawlings's administration had often viewed with skepticism (Akonor 2013). Kufuor shifted road spending away from rural areas in the north, instead choosing to improve the roads connecting Accra–Kumasi and Accra–Cape Coast, both of which supported him in the 2000 election. Kufuor's

---

[1] As IMF programs normally require some sort of adjustment (whether quantitative or structural), we use "IMF programs" and "IMF Structural Adjustment Programs" (SAPs) interchangeably.

administration also installed partisans in many of the country's parastatal organizations.

Some 2,500 miles away from the Ghanaian capital we see similar changes in the implementation of the ongoing IMF program in Kenya. President Moi seated in Nairobi relied upon a relatively narrow support base, primarily the Kalenjin ethnic group and other minor groups from Kenya's Rift Valley. Part of the IMF program required the government to slash the civil service by over 32,000 employees (Kamau 2000). Evidence of politically driven retrenchment emerged. Rules around dismissal favored the two largest ethnic groups – including President Moi's Kalenjin group – to the detriment of less powerful groups in the country (Otieno 2009). National Labor Party chairman Kennedy Kiliku said the retrenchment process was illegal, arguing that "opposition sympathizers were being victimized through retrenchment" (Kithi 2000). President Moi appeared less concerned about the protest that these choices engendered because they often came from opposition-supporting areas of the country. In comparison, when President Kibaki came to power with his broader coalition, he was much more sensitive to the potential for protest that his policies would create. This was reflected in broad-based sectoral and infrastructure initiatives like those of President Rawlings. While Kibaki was also tasked with retrenching a further 24,000 workers (Githahu and Omanga 2003), he resisted calls to cut the civil service (Opiyo 2003b). Like Rawlings in Ghana, Kibaki spent more on civil-service wages than agreed upon with the IMF, even seeking to expand the civil service as part of his approach to distributional politics. Finally, he was keenly attuned to demands from the IMF that would have negative impacts on his support base, even if they would benefit the country. One example was his reluctance to liberalize the maize market in Kenya because it would negatively impact maize farmers in the north of the country, a locus of support for him. We explore these illustrative cases in more detail in Sections 4 and 5.

As seen in our examples, these different administrations implemented IMF agreements in ways that sought to protect their supporters from the costs of adjustment and rewarded them with more spending on infrastructure in their areas. In contrast, opposition supporters disproportionately faced the burdens of adjustment, especially through job losses and spending cuts. Our approach views partisanship as an important mediator to understand who benefits from IMF agreements and who is burdened with the costs of adjustment. Governments benefit their supporters and burden the opposition. Other research has examined how governments act as mediators of IMF policy pressures but have taken different approaches focusing on the role of veto players (Vreeland 2003), strong labor presence (Caraway, Rickard, and Anner 2012), and government popularity (Shim 2022). While this research helps to inform us about how domestic issues influence governments' behavior toward the IMF, it does not examine the consequences of these programs.

Many scholars examine the consequences of IMF "structural adjustment programs" (SAPs) for the economy, society, and politics. These programs seek to promote deep-seated reforms that would transform borrowing countries into liberal market economies (Kentikelenis and Babb 2019; Kentikelenis, Stubbs, and King 2016; Polak 1991). Researchers disagree on the effectiveness of the IMF on growth, some finding negative impacts (Dreher 2006), while others find the opposite (Bas and Stone 2014). There is more consistent evidence that IMF SAPs do not make countries more resilient against financial crises (Dreher and Walter 2010), but instead incentivize moral hazard (Lipscy and Lee 2019). Overall, researchers concur that IMF programs adversely affect the wellbeing of societies, including poverty, inequality, public education, and public health (Biglaiser and McGauvran 2022; Lang 2021; Nooruddin and Simmons 2006; Oberdabernig 2013; Stubbs et al. 2020b; Stubbs and Kentikelenis 2018). There is also evidence that IMF programs increase the incidence of civil war, coups d'état, and political instability, leading to more frequent human rights violations (Abouharb and Cingranelli 2007; Casper 2017; Dreher and Gassebner 2012; Hartzell, Hoddie, and Bauer 2010; Pion-Berlin 1983).

A wide array of research seeks to understand the distributional consequences of IMF programs. Qualitative research in political economy describes how IMF SAPs advance the economic fortunes of some groups while disadvantaging others (Haggard and Kaufman 1992; Haggard and Webb 1993; Nelson 1992; Pastor 1987; Waterbury 1992). Quantitative research examines the distributional consequences, including: reducing government spending on public-sector wages and employment (Rickard and Caraway 2019); reducing labor's share of income and redistributing it toward the owners of capital (Pastor 1987; Stubbs et al. 2022; Vreeland 2002); worsening inequality (Chletsos and Sintos 2022b; Forster et al. 2019; Garuda 2000; Lang 2021); reducing incomes of the poor (Biglaiser and McGauvran 2022; Garuda 2000; Stubbs et al. 2022); and increasing unemployment and increasing the costs of services that people face (Chletsos and Sintos 2022a). We agree with much of the existing discussion about the winners and losers of adjustment lending. It suggests that the IMF supports farmers to promote economic development, shifts resources away from urban areas indulged by the central government, reduces the size of bloated state bureaucracies, privatizes a range of state-owned enterprises, and liberalizes the rules for many other aspects of economic life (Bates 1993; Easterly 2005; Haggard and Kaufman 1992; Kentikelenis, Stubbs, and King 2016; Stiglitz 2002). Public-sector workers, civil servants, and the urban poor

4 *International Relations*

may be hurt by cuts in government welfare and assistance. Workers in state-owned enterprises may lose their jobs because of privatization and members of the economic elite may lose out from structural adjustment program reforms that seek to reduce rent-seeking opportunities. Existing studies indicate that adjustment programs have distributional consequences. We think these studies underplay the partisan role of governments as mediators of IMF policy pressures who amplify these distributional consequences by choosing whom to protect and who bears the costs of adjustment. Despite the wealth of knowledge generated by this existing research, significant gaps exist in our understanding of the distributional consequences of IMF lending.

Existing work tends to frame our understanding of these policy choices as one based upon interest group lines (Grossman and Helpman 1994). It is the impact of the outcomes of the competition between interest groups on national governments that subsequently influence the content of the IMF adjustment programs. The most powerful will have policy directed to their benefit (Johnson and Salop 1980; Pastor 1987; Vreeland 2003, 136). Walter's (2013) carefully crafted argument examines the distributional consequences of financial crises on voters and how governments respond to them. We find Walter's analysis important but think it underplays the partisan politics of adjustment. In contrast to Walter, we think that governments seek to cushion their supporters from the pain of financial crises and place burdens on opposition supporters. Narrower work that examines the consequences of IMF lending is either framed along the lines of labor versus capital (e.g., Pastor 1988; Vreeland 2002); along the continuum of inequality (Forster et al. 2019; Lang 2021; Oberdabernig 2013); or discusses the concentration of wealth and poverty in particular deciles of the population (e.g., Biglaiser and McGauvran 2022; Garuda 2000; Stubbs et al. 2022). Research has found that IMF lending improves the likelihood of democratic leaders surviving in office (Smith and Vreeland 2006). Their findings suggest that political leaders may seek to use these loans for political advantage. Other research links compliance and non-compliance with IMF lending to political survival (Akonor 2013).

We agree with existing work that report what may be a puzzling set of findings: IMF programs often worsen inequality and poverty but at least for democrats seem to be associated with an increased chance of retaining political power. While powerful interest groups are to be reckoned with, we think this line of argument underplays the need for governments to satisfy their coalition of supporters to maintain political power. Existing work does little to incorporate an explicit partisan alignment dimension to the distributional consequences of IMF lending. Rickard and Caraway (2019, 39) note how the public sector is a source of patronage and this feeds governments'

IMF Lending: Partisanship, Punishment, and Protest

understandable reluctance to retrench. However, we also know that public-sector conditions occurred in 1,599 out of 1,976 country-years under IMF programs in developing countries from 1980 to 2018. This means that 80.9 percent of these country-years had labor conditionality, indicating frequent use of these conditions by the IMF (Kentikelenis, Stubbs, and King 2016). This indicates that painful retrenchment often does take place. Reluctant governments may have little option but to retrench their public sector, but we think that they do so with an eye to political advantage whenever possible, by protecting their supporters and burdening the costs of opposition. In contrast to Rickard and Caraway (2019), we think that governments make strategic choices in how to implement the reforms largely within the monetary and fiscal envelope agreed upon with the IMF. For example, when governments face demands to reduce the size of the public sector, we argue they will seek to protect their supporters from most of these cuts.

Our work seeks to build on existing research to better understand how governments, once they have agreed on a package of reforms with the IMF, *choose* to implement these conditions, and what the consequences are for domestic stability. Here we are not interested in whether governments comply with IMF-mandated reforms, which has been examined in related work (Reinsberg, Stubbs, and Kentikelenis 2022). Instead, we focus on the distributional politics in the implementation of IMF SAPs. We know little about who pays the costs of adjustment and who is spared from that pain. In short, we know little about the local political economy of such programs and the ramifications for protest in countries under IMF programs. We contend that this kind of distributional politics is prevalent in developing economies: governments reward their supporters with state support and withhold it from those who support the opposition. We argue that this "politics of alignment" approach provides a more nuanced understanding of how governments utilize discretion in IMF programs to their advantage. Our argument helps to better understand how partisan alignment mediates who wins and who loses from IMF lending. Our research goes beyond interest group arguments to highlight the politics involved in how governments implement these programs, seeking political advantage by rewarding their supporters and placing the burdens of these programs on those who support the opposition. It allows us to consider which individuals win and lose from these programs and the individual implications of distributional politics: (i) how people evaluate both the IMF and their national governments and (ii) if the losers are more likely to protest. If our arguments are correct, we should find strong partisan differences in evaluations of the IMF, evaluations of incumbents, and willingness to protest even after controlling for alternative explanations.

This leads to our central set of questions: How do government and opposition supporters view adjustment lending programs? Do government supporters benefit more and lose out less from adjustment lending compared to opposition supporters? If so, how do these beneficiaries and losers of adjustment lending view these programs? Do beneficiaries have more favorable views of their national governments or the IMF? Are those with less favorable evaluations of IMF adjustment more likely to protest? How do governments allocate the burdens and benefits of adjustment programs sponsored by the IMF? Do governments reward their supporters with the economic spoils of IMF adjustment programs while also protecting them from many of the burdens that come with such agreements? In contrast, do governments lump the burdens of these reform programs and their associated economic austerity on partisan supporters of the opposition? We have limited empirical understanding of the local and individual distributional effects of these programs, except for a few informative case studies.

In this Element, we assume that governments seek political advantage, especially during economically turbulent times. We posit that governments have more discretion than previous research has acknowledged about how they allocate not only the burdens but also the benefits of these reform programs within their societies. We argue that governments allocate adjustment burdens strategically to protect their partisan supporters, imposing adjustment costs upon the partisan supporters of their opponents, who then protest in response. To better understand the domestic political economy of these government choices, we shift attention to the micro-level experiences of hardship and local perceptions of the distributional effects of IMF programs. We argue that this micro-level perspective provides a much closer connection between governments' policy choices and individuals' experiences of IMF lending compared to national-level aggregates. As governments face more policy conditions from the IMF, which require more changes in their economies, we argue that they will have more discretion about how to achieve these targets. Our argument might seem counterintuitive to some observers of the adjustment lending process: as governments face more policy conditions from the IMF, they have greater scope for inflicting pain on their opponents while avoiding harm to their supporters.

Governments use their discretion within such programs to allocate associated economic burdens strategically through what we call the "politics of alignment." This approach highlights how governments utilize their policy levers to favor individuals and groups aligned with them to the detriment of those individuals and groups who support the opposition. As a result of such distributional politics, we expect to find highly unequal individual experiences of

IMF Lending: Partisanship, Punishment, and Protest

hardship and perceptions of the same country-level IMF program, along partisan lines. Government supporters will differ in their experiences of these programs and face fewer hardships than those who support the opposition. We expect opposition supporters to have worse experiences with these programs, face greater hardship, and protest more compared to those who support the government. Our analyses provide evidence that is consistent with the argument that governments under IMF adjustment programs act strategically to protect and benefit their supporters during economically turbulent times. Both our qualitative case studies, which leverage within-case variation, and our econometric analyses using individual survey data from around the world indicate that opposition supporters have more negative experiences of IMF lending, face more economic hardships, and protest more than supporters of the government. A striking feature of the large-N analysis is the consistency with which we find increased partisan gaps in perceptions and experiences of hardships and protest under IMF programs in the regional datasets – Afrobarometer (1999–2001), Asian Barometer (2005–8), and Latinobarometer (2005) – as well as the global longitudinal World Values Survey dataset (1981–2019). The results from our quantitative analysis are robust to a variety of alternative explanations, modeling specifications, and alternative econometric models.

Our work makes several contributions to the literature. We highlight the importance of partisanship as a key channel that influences individuals' experiences of IMF lending and their willingness to protest. In the context of distributional politics, partisanship helps us to understand not only whom governments seek to benefit from IMF lending (their supporters) but also how they punish opposition supporters with the costs of adjustment. Governments that face more conditions from the IMF have more flexibility in choosing how to protect their supporters and punish those who support the opposition while meeting benchmarks agreed upon with the IMF. We are the first to analyze large-N micro-level survey data from three world regions through a distributional lens to understand the local political economy of IMF lending. Our findings indicate that partisanship is an important predictor of people's varying experience of IMF lending and provides a micro-level explanation for macro-level phenomena like growing inequality under IMF SAPs. They help us better understand the partisan nature of who are the winners and losers from adjustment lending.

We highlight three of our key survey barometer findings, each consistent with the behavioral implications of strategic governments using the discretion that comes with IMF programs to protect their supporters and punish those who support the opposition. First, in countries under IMF programs, opposition supporters are more likely to report that the IMF SAP made their life worse than government supporters and compared to countries without IMF exposure.

Second, the partisan gap in these IMF SAP evaluations widens in IMF program countries with an above-median number of conditions compared to those countries facing a below-median number of conditions and is consistent with the argument that opposition supporters face heavier adjustment burdens. Finally, opposition supporters who report that the SAP made their lives worse are more likely to protest. Our models remain robust to a range of alternative explanations. Our findings highlight partisanship as an important predictor of different experiences and evaluations of SAPs. Our findings nuance sectoral and class-based explanations, which underplay the role of partisanship in explaining the winners and losers from adjustment and who protest these policies. Our findings suggest individuals within and across different sectors could fare better or worse depending upon if they support the government or the opposition. The theoretical importance of our work is to highlight that governments have much greater leverage than previously thought in their role as purveyors of IMF economic reforms. They shape the consequences of adjustment lending – benefiting their supporters and punishing those individuals who support the opposition.

2 Theoretical Framework

Our approach uses a novel distributional politics lens to systematically understand how individuals vary in their experience of IMF lending, which is different from almost all the existing work in this area. To inform our approach we draw upon several unconnected literature streams. First, the literature on patronage politics helps us to understand governments as strategic actors that use rewards and punishments to retain office (Kitschelt and Wilkinson 2007; Kopecký, Mair, and Spirova 2012; Kramon and Posner 2013; Panizza, Peters, and Ramos Larraburu 2019). As we detail consistently throughout this Element, government supporters have better access to government services, government jobs, access to food, potable water, healthcare, and education in comparison to opposition supporters. However, this literature has not yet answered whether and how submission to IMF SAPs affects the scope for distributional politics by governments.

Second, political economy literature on IMF SAPs has examined the causes and consequences of IMF SAPs for a range of socioeconomic outcomes, as well as conditions for country compliance with IMF SAPs (Reinsberg, Stubbs, and Kentikelenis 2021, 2022; Rickard and Caraway 2019; Stone 2002). Much of this work is based on large-N country-level analysis. Some earlier work uses case studies to analyze the distributive politics of IMF program implementation (Haggard and Kaufman 1992; Nelson 1984; Reno 1996). This literature leads us to think that people will have different experiences of IMF lending, but it lacks systematic micro-level evidence on individuals' perceptions and experiences with IMF SAPs.

Third, to understand how governments use externally sourced revenues for political advantage, we incorporate insights from the burgeoning subnational foreign aid literature, which shows that governments can use aid for political gain (Briggs 2014; Dreher et al. 2022; Isaksson and Kotsadam 2018; Jablonski 2014). This literature is replete with examples of distributional politics in the context of foreign aid. While the literature has focused on how governments allocate the spoils of aid as a source of unearned income, we consider the individual-level implications. Government supporters will benefit from these distributional choices about where to locate foreign aid projects. Nevertheless, this research lacks comparable analysis for how they allocate the burdens of adjustment, which we focus on.

Finally, we extend the implications of our individual-level distributional politics approach to the analysis of protest in the context of IMF adjustment lending. There is substantial literature linking IMF SAPs with protest, civil conflict, political instability, human rights repression, and coups d'état (Abouharb and Cingranelli 2009; Almeida and Pérez-Martin 2022; Casper 2017; Dreher and Gassebner 2012; Hartzell, Hoddie, and Bauer 2010; Keen 2005; Walton and Ragin 1990). For the literature that examines whether IMF programs engender protests, the findings are surprisingly mixed (Abouharb and Cingranelli 2007; Almeida and Pérez-Martin 2022; Auvinen 1996; Ortiz and Béjar 2013). We believe that this is also because the related large-N literature – with its focus on the country-year level – suffers from over-aggregation bias, concealing within-country variation in protest and asymmetric patterns of mobilization. The central tenets of IMF programs – deregulation, privatization of state assets, and civil-service retrenchment – intersect with many key drivers of conflict (Casper 2017; Hartzell, Hoddie, and Bauer 2010; Keen 2005). Yet, we have limited systematic knowledge about who protests and if individuals' experience of IMF SAPs influences their likelihood of protest. The existing literature almost invariably focuses on national-level analysis even if the mechanisms driving people to protest occur at the individual level. We need to better understand how IMF adjustment lending links to individuals' dispositions toward protest in the context of the state as a strategic mediator of the IMF's demands. Our approach is the first to consider if differences in perceptions and experiences with IMF SAPs depend upon whether individuals support the incumbent regime or opposition parties and if those differences result in more protest.

We begin by introducing the literature on patronage politics, which we extend with insights from research on the local political economy of foreign aid.

We then discuss the literature on the implementation of SAPs, to better understand how distributional politics shapes who is protected from the pain of adjustment reforms and who is burdened with the costs of these programs. This provides the basis for our expectations about the different experiences of IMF lending depending upon if individuals support the government or the opposition. We then link how these different experiences of IMF lending change the likelihood of protest.

2.1 The Politics of Alignment

A voluminous literature examines patronage politics where politicians provide a pick-and-mix range of goods including private goods, club goods, and programmatic ones to reward existing supporters and in some cases coax new ones to the fold (Harris and Posner 2019; Kitschelt and Wilkinson 2007; Kramon and Posner 2013; Panizza, Peters, and Ramos Larraburu 2019). At the heart of patronage is a clientelist exchange whereby incumbents provide goods to their supporters. These exchanges are especially relevant in information-poor developing countries because they guarantee voters access to benefits that they may not obtain otherwise in elections where politicians make programmatic promises (Chandra 2007; Kitschelt and Wilkinson 2007; van de Walle 2001).

Patronage politics is particularly prominent in sub-Saharan Africa. Built upon inter-elite bargains under authoritarian rule (Mwenda and Tangri 2005; van de Walle 2001; Warf 2017), it remains an important tool for politicians after democratization (Bratton and van de Walle 1997; Kopecký, Mair, and Spirova 2012; van de Walle 2007). Patronage exists across different institutional contexts, such as federalist states and unitarist states (Kopecký 2011), and extends well beyond sub-Saharan Africa, to include countries in Europe and Latin America (Kopecký et al. 2016; Oliveros 2021; Panizza, Peters, and Ramos Larraburu 2019; Szarzec, Totleben, and Pikatek 2022).

In the African context, the politics of alignment is often also along co-ethnic lines, as the existing distributional literature suggests (Carlitz 2017; Ejdemyr, Kramon, and Robinson 2018; Poulton and Kanyinga 2014; Theisen, Strand, and Østby 2020). Previous research argues that ethnicity is a heuristic for politicians to use when doling out benefits to groups and for individual voters to coalesce around to make their voices heard (Chandra 2007). Patronage politics can occur through civil-service appointments (Brierley 2021), infrastructure projects (Harding 2015), and welfare programs (Harris and Posner 2019; Kramon and Posner 2013). Government supporters consistently fare better than those who support the opposition concerning access to healthcare, education, civil-service jobs, and even potable water. While patronage extends deep into the civil

IMF Lending: Partisanship, Punishment, and Protest 11

service of some African countries, it is remarkably prevalent in different parts of the civil service and across levels of seniority (Kopecký 2011). Kopecký (2011, 724) ruefully describes the situation in both Ghana and South Africa:

> [P]arties in both countries uniformly appoint people to the highest positions in all ministries (i.e. chief directors and their deputies in Ghana, and director generals and their deputies in South Africa), and very often, especially in Ghana, also interfere in the appointment of the middle ranks within the ministries (i.e. heads of sections and other such positions). I use the term "interfere" deliberately in this context because in both countries most appointments to the ministerial bureaucracy outside the top level are supposed to be apolitical ... In practice, parties in both countries have managed to find loopholes in procedures and consequently have discovered ways to politicise appointments within the ministries to a much larger extent than the law permits.

Political leaders use senior appointments in the public sector to reward allies with offices that they can use to enrich themselves. This waterfall of patronage from one level of seniority to the next allows appointees to reward their networks in clientelist exchanges (van de Walle 2001). Again, we would expect these exchanges to benefit supporters of the government compared to the opposition.

Patronage politics flourishes where governments have access to significant sources of unearned income. Literature on the local distributional politics of foreign aid finds that governments engage in distributional politics, with political leaders dispensing aid to their supporters (Briggs 2014; Dreher et al. 2022; Isaksson and Kotsadam 2018; Jablonski 2014). Leaders send monies to their birth regions, especially in competitive elections (Dreher et al. 2022, 165). Allocation of multilateral development banks' project aid goes to constituencies with higher vote shares for the incumbent and co-ethnics (Jablonski 2014, 295). Earlier case-study research found evidence of biased allocation of public goods along partisan lines as part of the structural adjustment process (Herbst 1990; Keen 2005; Reno 1996; Zack-Williams 1999). We contend that governments make the same distributional choices in the context of IMF SAPs, rewarding their supporters where they retain discretion in how they comply with IMF demands.

Politicians have a good idea of who their voters are, where they live, and act to reward them individually. They target spending geographically, even within their constituencies, to reward voters for their collective support (Chandra 2007; Harris and Posner 2019; Oliveros 2021). If government parties know who their voters are, where they live, and how to reward them, we would expect that they also know whom to target with the burden of adjustment when facing austerity

12 *International Relations*

pressures. To date, however, there is limited evidence on how governments that engage in patronage politics respond to pressures for adjustment. To better understand how IMF SAPs affect patronage politics, we first need to understand the purpose of these programs.

2.2 The Politics of Alignment under IMF Adjustment Programs

Countries in dire economic straits often turn to the IMF for emergency loans. Under IMF auspices, governments often implement fiscal austerity to bring their financial house in order, which should help restore investor confidence, avert financial crises, and restore economic growth (Bas and Stone 2014; Dreher 2006; Lipscy and Lee 2019). A large country-level literature has examined how IMF SAPs affect socioeconomic outcomes such as economic growth, debt, health, income inequality, and government spending (Lang 2021; Nooruddin and Simmons 2006; Oberdabernig 2013; Stubbs et al. 2020b; Stubbs and Kentikelenis 2018).

In addition to austerity measures, governments under IMF SAPs must often embark on structural reforms that seek to overhaul the entire domestic political economy (Easterly 2005; Reinsberg, Kern, and Rau-Göhring 2021; Vreeland 2003). IMF adjustment programs liberalize markets, privatize state assets, and retrench the state (Babb 2013; Kentikelenis, Stubbs, and King 2016; Stone 2002). An oft-cited official rationale for structural reforms is to weaken patronage networks, benefit farmers in the rural economy, and encourage export-led economic growth (Bates 1993; Tait 1989; Vreeland 2003). As long argued by the political economy literature, IMF SAPs have built-in distributional consequences that favor some groups but disadvantage other groups, and these distributional effects have repercussions for the implementation of IMF SAPs (Haggard and Kaufman 1992; Nelson 1984; Reno 1996; Zack-Williams 1999). Following their lead, we argue that political leaders face a set of potentially competing demands from different individuals and groups: they need to credibly satisfy the IMF to keep funds flowing; they need to respond to organized lobbies; and they need to enact policy choices to garner themselves enough support for re-election or to retain political power. The last is of particular interest to us.

Considering their continued incentives for patronage politics, we expect governments will lump adjustment burdens on opposition supporters while trying to protect their own supporters. If politicians know whom to hire and where to spend money to reward their supporters – as demonstrated by the literature on patronage politics and the local politics of foreign aid – they will also know whom to fire in the public sector and which public services to cut to target individuals and constituencies who do not support them. We then expect that government supporters will have different experiences of these IMF programs compared to those who support the opposition.

An important consideration is whether governments have enough discretion for distributive politics when they are under IMF tutelage. While cross-country research has examined government discretion in the adjustment process (Beazer and Woo 2015; Nooruddin and Simmons 2006; Stone 2002; Vreeland 2003), conventional wisdom would expect decreasing scope for distributive politics when governments need to make cuts. For example, Kentikelenis, Stubbs, and King (2016) describe how governments lost policy space with the IMF-led expansion of structural adjustment lending. However, this declining policy space does not mean that governments have no discretion about how to implement IMF policy conditions. As we argue below, more conditions that affect wider swathes of the economy will leave governments with even more room to achieve their partisan goals while meeting the demands of the IMF.

Even though IMF SAPs regularly contain macroeconomic targets for tax revenue, public spending, and public-sector employment, they do not specify which groups and individuals to retrench in the public sector or whom to target with cuts to welfare spending. Governments thus retain some discretion in how they comply with IMF conditions, and we contend they use this flexibility for their political advantage. By targeting their political opponents and opposition supporters with the costs of adjustment, governments under IMF programs can still fulfill adjustment targets. If decision-makers utilize this process to protect and even possibly reward their supporters while placing the burdens of adjustment on opposition supporters, we should observe a divergence in perceptions and experiences of IMF SAPs across partisan lines. This leads us to expect that partisan supporters of the government view the consequences of IMF program lending less negatively than partisans who supported the opposition.

We consider that government discretion in IMF SAPs is not uniform. We expect to find particularly strong evidence for distributive politics in sectors of the economy under government control (Haggard and Kaufman 1992; Nelson 1984; Waterbury 1992). We pay particular attention to those employed in the public sector – arguably the sector in which the government has more immediate and direct control over both the appointment and retention of its supporters (Brierley 2021; Haggard and Kaufman 1992; Kopecký 2011; Nelson 1984; Waterbury 1992). For example, as part of any agreed IMF SAP, governments may choose to close particular government offices in opposition-held districts or re-route investment or subsidies to regions that supported the government. The largest group who we think will be protected from most cuts will be government employees, especially when these groups disproportionately support the incumbent administration. This leads us to expect that the partisan gap in experience and evaluation of IMF lending will be even larger in the public sector between supporters of the government compared to those who support the opposition.

Finally, we argue that as the number of policy conditions increases so do the potential adjustment burdens that governments can allocate to supporters of the opposition. Our notion of government discretion is different from existing uses in the literature on IMF SAPs. While we emphasize discretion concerning how governments choose to locally implement policy conditions, existing literature has distinguished different types of conditionality (Biglaiser and McGauvran 2022; IMF 2001b; Reinsberg, Kentikelenis, and Stubbs 2019; Woo 2013). On the one hand, quantitative conditions target macroeconomic aggregates such as budget deficits, tax revenues, debt service, and inflation, leaving governments discretion in how they reach those targets. Decision-makers then retain wide discretion over the localized micro-decisions that ensure they meet aggregate targets, including which taxes to impose, which public services to cut, and which civil servants to dismiss. On the other hand, structural conditions include measures such as privatizing state-owned enterprises, reforming welfare, and pension systems, liberalizing trade policies, or restructuring tax systems (Kentikelenis et al. 2016; Stubbs et al. 2020a; Woo 2013). These types of conditions specify overall aims and policy instruments, thereby reducing the range of instruments available in the implementation of IMF SAPs (Fernández-I-Marín, Knill, and Steinebach 2021). Nonetheless, we expect that governments retain discretion in the implementation of structural conditions too. Our case studies provide evidence of how governments managed the privatization process to benefit their supporters and rigged civil-service reforms to punish opposition supporters.

In sum, we argue that governments retain a margin of discretion over how they implement IMF conditions at the local level. Across different types of conditions, governments seek to exploit their discretion to benefit government supporters while harming opposition supporters. Governments can target these individuals directly when they have information about their identity, for instance from party member lists. They may also use spatial tactics of distributive politics, designing policies that favor individuals in government-held areas, while harming individuals in opposition strongholds (Appiah-Kubi 2001; Briggs 2014; Campos and Esfahani 1996). In any case, the scope for distributive politics increases with the number of conditions included in an IMF SAP. As governments face a higher number of conditions in an IMF SAP, the potential amount of burden they can use to punish opposition supporters increases. We expect that incumbent governments use this increased scope for their political

IMF Lending: Partisanship, Punishment, and Protest

advantage, punishing their opponents while avoiding harm to their supporters. As a result, we expect to find more unequal experiences across partisan lines in countries under IMF SAPs with more conditions.

2.3 Public Goods Provision, IMF SAPs, and Protest

In this section, we argue that unequal experiences of IMF SAPs because of distributive politics can affect protest. To that end, we link two hitherto unconnected streams of literature. The first discusses the link between unequal public goods provision and protest. The second examines the effects of IMF SAPs on political instability and protest. Neither literature provides a micro-level distributional politics understanding of how IMF programs increase protest by amplifying pre-existing inequalities within states. Taken together they do help to shed light on how biased implementation of IMF SAPs serves to increase protest.

Inequality of public goods provision can drive protest. Some are "service delivery protests" or "valence protests," which focus on the pursuit of material goods and are not ideological or revolutionary in character (Bond and Mottiar 2013; Harris and Hern 2019; Harsch 2009; Trasberg 2021). These studies document a range of protest triggers, which include the removal of subsidies for food and fuel, poor provision of public services, complaints about police conduct, limited and substandard housing and medical care, as well as the imposition of school fees. In other cases where governments cut the size and scope of the state for reasons of ideology and fiscal consolidation, protests often become part of larger ideological struggles against neoliberalism (Almeida and Pérez-Martin 2022; Bond 1998; Branch and Mampilly 2015; Collins 1988; Ellis and Van Kessel 2008; Mueller 2013). While we learn a lot from this research about the inequality of public goods provision and protest, limitations remain in our understanding of this link.

The existing qualitative research does not provide us with a systematic micro-level explanation of the role distributional politics plays in who protests and why (Bond 1988; Bond and Mottiar 2013; Ellis and Van Kessel 2008). While research on subnational protest (Almeida and Pérez-Martin 2022; Arce and Mangonnet 2013) or surveys of citizens and local elites about the reasons for protest (Harris and Hern 2019; Harsch 2009; Trasberg 2021) provide us with more systematic information about the drivers of protest, we still lack a micro-level understanding of how distributional politics shapes protest behavior.

Another set of studies examines the link between IMF SAPs and protests (Abouharb and Cingranelli 2007; Almeida and Pérez-Martin 2022; Auvinen 1996; Bienen and Gersovitz 1985; Ortiz and Béjar 2013; Payer 1975; Sidell 1988). The findings from this literature are surprisingly mixed. While research

16 *International Relations*

links adjustment lending to more anti-government protests, riots, and even episodes of rebellion (Abouharb and Cingranelli 2007; Almeida and Pérez-Martin 2022; Hartzell, Hoddie, and Bauer 2010; Walton and Ragin 1990), other work finds little support for the contention that adjustment lending leads to more protest (Auvinen 1996; Bienen and Gersovitz 1985; Payer 1974; Sidell 1988).

Two limitations of this literature can account for these mixed findings. While we cannot entirely dismiss the findings of previous national-level research indicating no effect between IMF programs and protest, we think it masks important subnational variation. Following the logic of our politics of alignment argument, biased implementation of IMF SAPs by governments may mobilize some groups and demobilize others, leaving aggregate protest unchanged. Second, almost all discussions of the protest-inducing effects of IMF SAPs are detached from partisan politics. While research links protest to those who lose from IMF SAPs due to austerity, retrenchment, and privatization (Abouharb and Cingranelli 2007; Hartzell, Hoddie, and Bauer 2010; Walton and Ragin 1990), this is without reference to partisan politics. More recent contributions are no exception. For example, Almeida and Pérez-Martin (2022) carefully analyze resistance to neoliberalism, describing how social movements emerge from groups who lose from adjustment lending but do not examine how governments' strategic implementation of SAPs may drive protest by burdening opposition supporters with the costs of adjustment.

We seek to address these gaps by arguing in the next section that governments act as strategic mediators of IMF policy demands. Governments' biased implementation of policies agreed upon with the IMF is an important driver of protest by opposition supporters who experience higher costs of adjustment compared to government supporters.

2.4 Distributional Politics and Protest in the Context of IMF Lending

We argue that the role of IMF adjustment lending in many societies amplifies pre-existing distributional inequalities because SAPs reduce the fiscal headroom of governments and typically demand unpopular cuts in expenditure and agonizing economic reforms. Governments facing IMF adjustment pressures will then have to decide how they implement SAPs. We argue that governments – seeking to maintain their winning coalition to retain political power (Bueno de Mesquita et al. 2003) – lump adjustment burdens on supporters of the political opposition while trying to protect their partisans. We expect that this amplification of distributional politics under IMF adjustment lending will lead opposition supporters to protest more.

IMF Lending: Partisanship, Punishment, and Protest

Our argument builds on four key insights from the previous literature. First, in line with previous research on IMF SAP implementation, we conceive governments as strategic actors responding to the demands of the IMF and their domestic lobbies in their choices about when they go under adjustment lending, the range of policy changes they agree to, and their degree of implementation with agreed targets (Nooruddin and Simmons 2006; Rickard and Caraway 2019; Stone 2002; Vreeland 2003). Second, as demonstrated by the rich literature on subnational distributional politics (Beiser-McGrath, Müller-Crepon, and Pengl 2020; Carlitz 2017; Ejdemyr, Kramon, and Robinson 2018), governments seek political advantage in the distribution of state resources. Especially in information-poor developing countries, incumbent governments rely on clientelist networks to hold onto power (Chandra 2007). Governments can either identify their supporters directly and reward them with lucrative jobs in the civil service (Brierley 2021; Kitschelt and Wilkinson 2007; Kopecký 2011) or they know the spatial distribution of their support base, and allocate public goods to their support base but not to opposition-held areas (Harding 2015; Harris and Posner 2019; Kramon and Posner 2013). Third, IMF SAPs have redistributive effects baked into their formulation that can trigger political unrest. The central tenets of these programs – civil-service retrenchment, privatization of state-owned enterprises, and market liberalization – intersect with many key drivers of conflict (Casper 2017; Hartzell, Hoddie, and Bauer 2010; Keen 2005). Fourth, governments' dealings with external actors can amplify their capacity for distributional politics. The local political economy of foreign aid literature indicates that governments use aid to advantage their supporters, often to the detriment of opposition-held areas (Anaxagorou et al. 2020; Briggs 2014; Dreher et al. 2019; Jablonski 2014; Lio 2020).

Combining insights from these literature streams, we expect distributive politics to intensify when countries go under IMF SAPs. While foreign aid allows governments to increase resource transfers to their supporters, IMF SAPs do not create the same fiscal space, but rather require governments to cut expenditures and undergo painful reforms. Under IMF SAPs, distributional politics takes a different form in that governments will allocate adjustment burdens to opposition supporters while shielding their supporters as much as possible. Governments thereby amplify the distributional impact of global policy pressures inscribed into IMF SAPs. This intensification of distributional politics in the wake of IMF SAPs can lead to increased protest.

As we know from the vast literature on protest and social movements, individuals need to be aggrieved, mobilized, and have political opportunity structures for protest to occur (Almeida 2019; Gurr 1969; Olson 1971; Tarrow 1996; Tilly 1978). Austerity may not cause protest unless its actual or perceived implementation is unequal and generates sufficient grievances to mobilize people. For example, Reinsberg and Abouharb (2022) discuss the case of Grenada where over the period 2013–14 the Mitchell administration negotiated a homegrown SAP with the IMF. The package involved a series of uncomfortable economic reforms that could have sparked protest. These included spending cuts, removal of many exemptions and subsidies, limited increases in public-sector pay and pensions, and lowered tax allowances. Yet the program was not met by waves of protest witnessed elsewhere in the Caribbean. The government widely engaged stakeholders on the form of the agreement, stated that the economic reforms would be undertaken progressively with measures that exempted the most vulnerable, and refused to retrench the civil service. This mix of engagement, perceived fairness, and protection for the most vulnerable groups in society prevented protests from taking root against the administration.

This example illustrates our general argument that IMF conditions may not cause grievances and protest on their own but also require governments to act in a way that gives citizens reasons to believe they have not been treated equally in the process. Considering that cases such as Grenada are rare, our general expectation is that governments will implement IMF SAPs to their political advantage, without necessarily being concerned about the consequences for protest. Extending the logic of governments as strategic actors, who wish to retain their winning coalition (Bueno de Mesquita et al. 2003), we argue that where governments face pressures for adjustment, they will try to implement them in a way that maximizes their chances of political survival. We, therefore, expect governments to lump the burdens of conditionality on opposition supporters. For example, governments facing conditions to cut the numbers employed in the civil service will retrench civil servants aligned with opposition parties, and bend rules and procedures to cuts wages, welfare, and pensions, so the costs fall disproportionally on opposition supporters. Empirical evidence from Kenya – discussed later in this Element – confirms this expectation. Our discussion leads us to expect that IMF adjustment lending amplifies partisan-biased distributional politics increasing the frequency of protests by opposition supporters compared to those who support the government. We expect that the effects will be even more pronounced in countries where the IMF SAPs have many conditions because they provide governments with more opportunities to lump the burdens of adjustment lending on supporters of the opposition.

We argue that governments are well placed to understand the potential consequences of their actions which will likely lead opposition supporters to protest more. We also argue that governments may well view this as "a cost of doing business." Governments may expect protests from the usual suspects in

IMF Lending: Partisanship, Punishment, and Protest   19

the opposition and discount their importance because they have been able to preserve the support of their winning coalition. It is much more problematic for governments if they cannot maintain their coalitions and the situation breaks down into mass political protest that threatens the survival of government in office (Bueno de Mesquita and Smith 2010; Casper and Tyson 2014; Magaloni and Wallace 2008). Our distributional politics approach helps to explain some previous findings that even large-scale protests often fail to change the course of government policy (Almeida and Pérez-Martin 2022). We argue that *who protests* matters to the government, especially if they take a distributional approach to the benefit and burdens of adjustment lending, they may well expect opposition supporters to rally against these new injustices. However, this matters little if the government keeps its winning coalition together to remain in office (Bueno de Mesquita et al. 2003).

In the section that follows we describe the data that we will use in our large-N micro-level analyses, which we think provides a close test of the implications of our argument. We begin with descriptive data of participation in IMF programs by region over time and examine people's evaluations of IMF SAPs, indicators of satisfaction with public goods provision, levels of protest, and degrees of partisan affiliation. We finish with a brief discussion about the estimation techniques we use to analyze the link between IMF programs and distributive politics in Section 4 and then how distributive politics under IMF lending affects protest in Section 5.

3 Data

3.1 Survey Data

We draw on individual-level data from three regional barometer surveys – the first wave of the Afrobarometer (1999–2001), the second wave of the Asian Barometer (2005–8), and the tenth wave of the Latinobarometer (2005) – as well as the longitudinal World Values Survey (1981–2019) dataset. We choose these surveys because they allow us to cast light on our research questions from various angles.

A key benefit of using the three regional surveys is that we can draw on multiple pieces of evidence that jointly corroborate the implications of our theoretical argument on the distributive politics of IMF program implementation. Considering the difficulties of accurately measuring distributive politics, we believe that triangulating observational evidence from many different sources holds promise to strengthen our findings. While the Afrobarometer measures respondent evaluations of IMF SAPs, the other barometers help us arbitrate competing explanations for why such evaluations exist. For example, the Asian Barometer measures both confidence in the IMF and individual perceptions of unbiased policy implementation by the government. The Latinobarometer includes questions about respondent perceptions of the quality of public services which are often targeted by structural adjustment programs. These various survey items, therefore, hold the potential to enrich our picture of the distributive politics of structural adjustment. Finally, by using the combined longitudinal World Values Survey data, we probe the generalizability of our findings to all world regions. Despite the unavailability of IMF-specific attitudinal measures and a less accurate measure of partisan allegiance, the World Values Survey dataset offers a robustness test of our argument using a common operationalization of our key variables. Its greater country-wave coverage also helps us obtain evidence to suggest that it is indeed IMF programs, rather than the financial turmoil that usually precedes them, which drive the differences in partisan gaps regarding experienced hardship and protest.

An additional advantage is that many countries during these survey periods underwent IMF programs. Figure 1 shows the number of countries with active programs in different world regions from 1980 to 2018. The survey waves that we examine in the Afrobarometer and the Latinobarometer fall within periods in which these countries made extensive use of IMF programs. For Asian countries, the use of IMF programs declined rapidly after the Asian Financial Crisis, following their reluctance to seek IMF assistance due to IMF stigma (Gehring and Lang 2020; Ito 2012; Lipscy and Lee 2019). Figure 2 further demonstrates

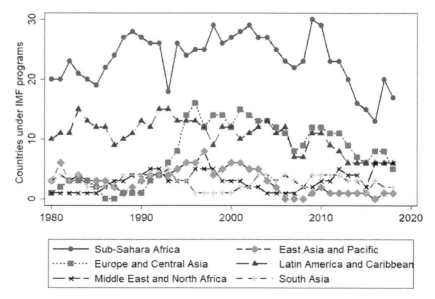

Figure 1 IMF program participation across different regions

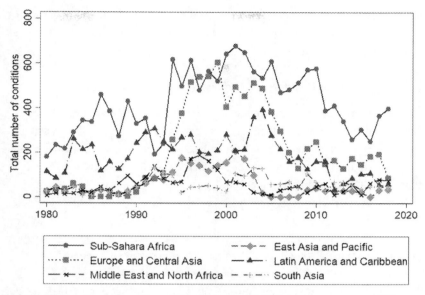

Figure 2 Total number of conditions in active IMF programs across different regions

that our survey periods coincide with times of high adjustment pressure. The number of conditions peaked around the turn of the Millennium for African countries and in the mid-2000s for Latin American countries. Asia had its heyday of structural adjustment before the 2000s.

Table A1 in the appendix shows the countries under IMF programs in each barometer. We drop high-income countries from the samples because our focus is on developing countries. This sampling choice also ensures that we compare countries that are structurally similar concerning the possibility of coming under an IMF program. This allows us to undertake plausible comparisons in survey responses between countries under IMF programs and countries not under IMF programs. In addition, by focusing on countries with exposure to IMF SAPs, we can exploit differences in IMF program design in terms of the number of IMF conditions (Kentikelenis, Stubbs, and King 2016).

3.2 Individual-Level Variables

Our goal is to understand how partisan allegiances affect respondent perceptions and evaluations of the socioeconomic effects of IMF SAPs as well as participation in protest. While all three barometer surveys include comparable questions on protest, the survey items on evaluations are worded differently. We focus on introducing these main outcomes. In the empirical sections, we lever additional outcomes helping to corroborate our evidence on distributive politics and to dismiss alternative explanations. We introduce these additional outcomes in the subsequent sections.

3.2.1 Perceptions and Experiences of Hardship

In the Afrobarometer survey, we measure how people perceive the IMF SAP of their country to have affected their personal economic circumstances. Comparativists refer to such assessments as *pocketbook evaluations*, which most respondents will find easy to answer as they can draw on their own experience (Duch and Stevenson 2006).

To capture pocketbook evaluations, we draw on the following Afrobarometer survey question: "What effect do you think [the SAP] has had on the way you live your life? Has it made it worse, had no effect, or made it better?" Answer categories include: "A lot worse," "worse," "neither better nor worse," "better," "a lot better," and separately, non-responses or missing data.

Figure 3 shows the distribution of pocketbook evaluations of IMF SAPs, available for individuals who have heard about the IMF SAP of their country. What is striking is that there is considerable heterogeneity in responses. While negative assessments of IMF SAPs dominate (59.9%), a sizable share of respondents say their economic circumstances slightly improved (19.3%); some respondents did not experience any difference (15.0%), and a small remainder improved significantly (5.9%). Considering that IMF SAPs are

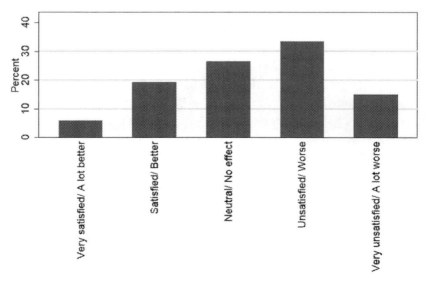

Figure 3 Distribution of pocketbook evaluations of IMF SAPs

IMF Lending: Partisanship, Punishment, and Protest

often portrayed as uniformly challenging in the policy discourse (Reinsberg, Stubbs, and Kentikelenis 2022), these patterns are remarkable and merit further investigation.

Figure A1 in the appendix plots the distribution of responses to this question separately for all countries in which it was asked. The variation in SAP evaluations is not driven by specific countries. In most countries, IMF SAP evaluations hover around the middle category. A clear exception is South Africa, where the modal experience with the IMF SAP seems to have been very negative. Zimbabwe is another case in which the modal experience has been negative. In Mali, relatively more people were satisfied with the IMF SAP. We confirm that SAP evaluations differ more within countries than across countries by decomposing variation in the outcome. This indicates a general pattern whereby IMF SAPs create both winners and losers, with the losers being in the relative majority.

Because the surveys for Asia and Latin America do not directly ask respondents about their perceptions of IMF SAPs, we need to draw on alternative evaluation questions. In the Asian Barometer, we have the unique opportunity to understand whom people blame for the possible deterioration of their economic circumstances. We draw on two related questions. The first asks respondents to evaluate the extent to which their government treats everyone equally or not: "Now I am going to read to you a list of statements that describe how people often feel about the state of affairs in [country]. Please tell me whether you strongly agree, somewhat agree, somewhat disagree, or strongly disagree with each of these statements: Everyone is treated equally by the government" (*Q108*). The second probes respondent evaluations of the IMF among those individuals who have heard about the organization: "Please let us know about your impression of the following organizations: the International Monetary Fund" (*Q163*). Answer categories are on a scale from 1 to 10, where 1 is "very bad" and 10 is "very good."

Figure 4 shows the distribution of responses for perceptions of government biasedness in Asian Barometer countries with exposure to IMF programs. People are divided in their views on whether their government treats people equally or not: 40 percent disagree with the statement that their government treats everyone equally (10 percent disagree even strongly), and almost 60 percent think their government is unbiased, while only a small percentage cannot judge either way. In the appendix, we find similar patterns concerning perceptions of government biasedness in all Asian program countries (Figure A2).

Figure 5 shows how people perceive the IMF. In contrast to their own governments, most people have a positive impression of the IMF: 60 percent give it a high rating of at least 7 out of 10 and fewer than 5 percent give a low rating of at most 3 out of 10. This result is somewhat surprising, given the bad reputation of the IMF,

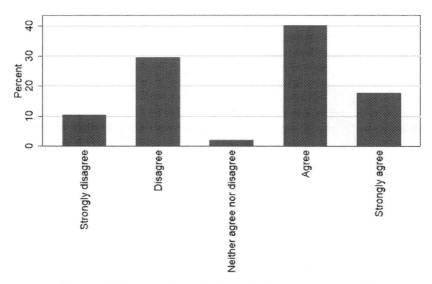

Figure 4 "Everyone is treated equally by the government"

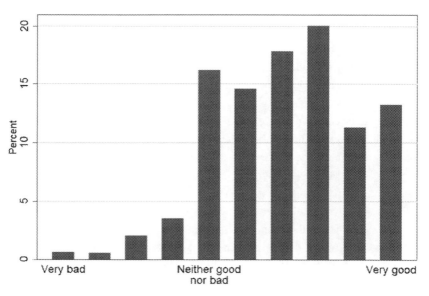

Figure 5 Impression of the IMF across Asian Barometer countries

especially in Asia after the Asian Financial Crisis (Ito 2012). In the appendix, we plot the distributions by country. We find similar patterns across program countries concerning perceptions of government bias, with a slightly higher perception that the government is biased in Mongolia (Figure A2) and impressions of the IMF, with slightly more IMF-critical views in Indonesia (Figure A3).

Like the Asian Barometer, the Latinobarometer does not ask respondents about their perceptions of the IMF SAP. Instead, the survey includes questions on the perceived quality of public services and their satisfaction with the functioning of the market economy. These are important issues because they are directly affected by IMF conditionality: an abundant literature documents how the IMF has agreed with governments on reforms that seek to reduce public spending, privatize public service provision and liberalize markets and prices (Babb 2013; Kentikelenis, Stubbs, and King 2016; Reinsberg et al. 2019; Rickard and Caraway 2019). To the extent that governments implement at least some of these reforms, we would expect their consequences to be felt by citizens, with changes in their perceptions of public service quality as a result.

We draw on two survey questions from the Latinobarometer asking respondents for their views of how the quality of public services has changed over the past year. The survey questions read as follows: "Would you say that in [country], in the last 12 months, the quality of the [public schools/public hospitals] has gone down, gone up or stayed the same?" (*P90STB/P90STA*). Answers on a five-point Likert scale include "has gone up a lot," "has gone up a little," "has stayed the same," "has gone down a little," "has gone down a lot," and separately, non-responses. For our purposes, these questions are advantageous because they allow us to compare how public service quality evolved in countries under IMF programs compared to countries not under such programs. This provides for stronger inferences compared to survey items that just capture the current level of satisfaction with public services and thus are missing an individual-level baseline. Moreover, this question wording is closest to the question in the Afrobarometer survey asking respondents to assess the IMF SAP.

The results show most people have experienced no change in how they perceive the quality of public services in their country. The remaining responses divide roughly equally between perceived improvements and perceived deteriorations in public schooling (Figure 6) and public hospitals (Figure 7). In the appendix, we further analyze current levels of satisfaction with public service provision, finding that respondents are exactly split as to whether they are satisfied or not with the quality of public schools in their country – both in the aggregate (Figure A4) and across individual countries (Figure A5). Similarly, people are divided on their perceived quality of public health services – both in the aggregate (Figure A6) and in individual countries (Figure A7).

Across all regional surveys, we have found considerable variation in how individuals assess the effects of IMF SAPs concerning their own fortunes and the quality of public-service provision, and whether or not they conceive governments as biased implementers of IMF-mandated reforms.

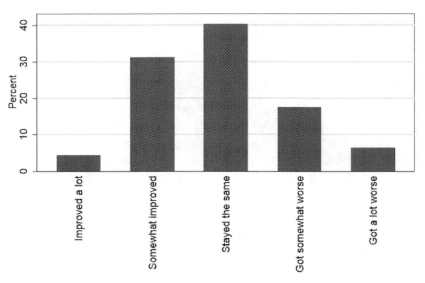

Figure 6 Evolution of perceived quality of public education in Latin American program countries

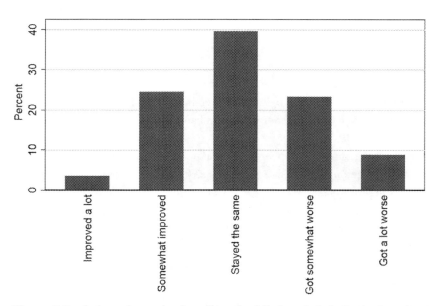

Figure 7 Evolution of perceived quality of public hospitals in Latin American program countries

In the World Values Survey, we can capture experiences of hardship through two measures. The first is an index of deprivation that draws on three items asking whether the respondent (and their family) have respectively gone without enough food to eat, gone without medicine or treatment, and gone without cash income in the past twelve months (*H008*). The frequency of each marker of deprivation can be: never (0), rarely (1), sometimes (2), or often (3). We create a deprivation index by adding up the categorical response values over all three types of deprivation. The resulting index can range from zero (never any deprivation in any dimension) to nine (often deprived for all three essential items). The second outcome is the income group of a respondent. Within each country, respondents can be in one of three income groups relative to the living standard in that country: low income, medium income, and high income (*X047CS*).

Figure 8 shows the prevalence of different forms of deprivation across all respondents of the World Values Survey. While over 40 percent of respondents never experienced any material hardship, almost 60 percent did experience some hardships during the year before the survey. Where they occurred, however, hardship experiences were relatively mild (for example, an index value of "one" means hardship was rare and only in one dimension). There are somewhat fewer respondents who sometimes or often experience hardship across more than one dimension. The most extreme form of deprivation – being deprived "often" of all three types of essential goods – is extremely rare (index value of "nine").

Figure 9 shows a range of income inequality across the respondents of all survey countries. Most people have a medium income. About one-third of the respondents have low incomes. About one-sixth of the respondents have high incomes.

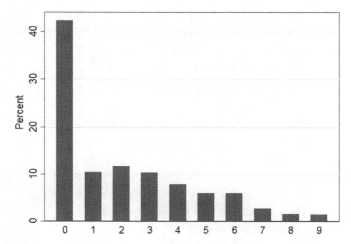

Figure 8 Prevalence of deprivation among respondents in the World Values Survey

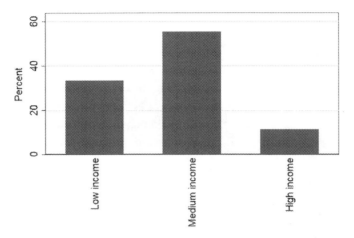

Figure 9 Income distribution of respondents in the World Values Survey

3.2.2 Protest

Our second outcome of interest is protest. Comparativists have debated how to measure protest in surveys, specifically whether to only measure protest behavior or also include protest inclination. On the one hand, only considering actual protest provides a conservative measurement strategy because it requires a behavioral response. On the other hand, capturing protest inclination could be advantageous because it likely is a first step toward actual protest. At the same time, protest inclination measures individual preferences not imbued by considerations about collective mobilization and potential repression of protest by the government that may discourage people from actually protesting (Ritter and Conrad 2016). We consider both measures substantively interesting. We proceed with actual protest because it is available in all surveys. For some surveys, we also use the inclusive measure that combines actual protest and protest inclination. Our results are not sensitive to this choice.

In the Afrobarometer, the corresponding survey question on protest is: "Here are a number of different actions people might take if government were to do something they thought was wrong or harmful. For each of these, please tell me whether you have engaged in this activity or not: Attend demonstration or protest march?" (*pardem*). This question has five answer categories, including "Yes, often," "Yes, a few times," "Yes, once," "No, but would do if I had the chance," and "No, would never do." Most people never protest, and only a few posit to have engaged in protest. A sizable share of about 10 percent would protest if given the chance (Figure 10). In the appendix, we plot the distribution

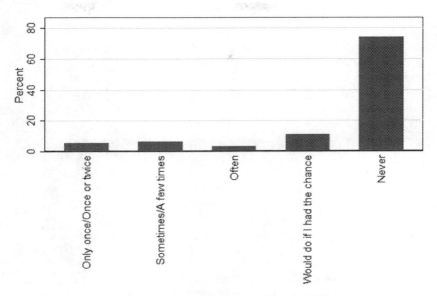

Figure 10 Protest in sub-Saharan African program countries

of responses separately for all countries in the survey (Figure A8). We obtain qualitatively similar patterns, suggesting that the protest results are unlikely to be driven by individual countries.

In the Asian Barometer, the protest question is somewhat simpler: "Did you attend a demonstration or protest march in the past twelve months?" ($Q88$). The four possible answer categories include "Yes, more than once," "Yes, once," "No, never," and non-responses. The drawback is that we cannot capture protest inclinations in the Asian Barometer. Instead, the survey includes a question on violent protest that can be used for robustness tests. Figure 11 shows the distribution of responses, indicating that protest is very uncommon in Asia: over 90 percent of the respondents have never protested. At the same time, protest (or lack thereof) is not unique to any Asian country in particular – the appendix shows similar patterns across all Asian program countries (Figure A9).

In the Latinobarometer, respondents are asked to indicate participation in a whole battery of contentious behaviors. The introductory text reads: "I am going to read out a political activity. I would like you to tell me, if you have ever done it, if you would ever do it, or if you would never do it?". This is followed by a list of activities including signing a petition; taking part in an authorized demonstration; participating in riots; occupying land, buildings, or factories; blocking traffic; taking part in unauthorized demonstrations; and contacting

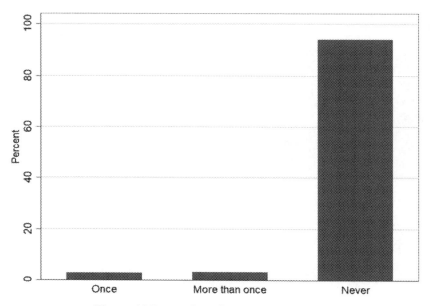

Figure 11 Protest in Asian program countries

officials, parliamentarians, or civil society actors. We do not use all these activities but focus on the items that are closest to protest. Hence, we include responses on authorized demonstrations, unauthorized demonstrations, and riots. Figure 12 shows the distribution of responses based on lawful demonstrations only – the type of activity with the most affirmative responses. In line with the other surveys, most people do not engage in protest, while some would consider doing so, and only a few have actually done so. In the appendix, we verify that these patterns look similar across Latin American program countries (Figure A10).

We have learned that a majority of individuals across all barometers have not engaged in protest. Comparing across regions, protest is more common in Latin America than in Asia, and slightly more common than in Africa. While only a minority has engaged in protest, significant proportions of respondents have a latent potential to do so.

In the World Values Survey, we measure whether respondents have engaged in a lawful protest in the past twelve months ($E221B$). Figure 13 plots the distribution of responses across all respondents, showing that about 24 percent have protested while 76 percent have not. Protest thus appears to be more prevalent in the global sample than in the regional barometers. It remains to be seen whether grievances induced by IMF-mandated reforms translate into greater inclinations for protest and protest behavior.

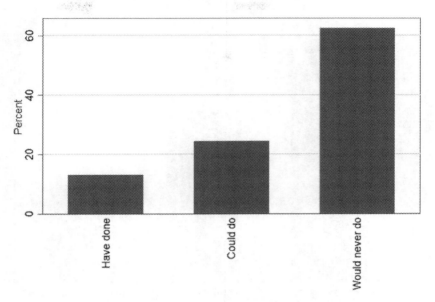

Figure 12 Protest in Latin American program countries

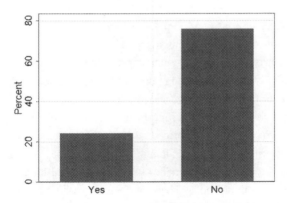

Figure 13 Protest among World Values Survey respondents

3.2.3 Partisan Allegiances

To test our argument, we require individual-level data on the partisan allegiance of respondents. The survey datasets differ concerning the extent to which they offer a straightforward measure of partisan allegiance, although we are always able to (re)construct these partisan allegiances using additional information (see Tables A4 and A5). The Afrobarometer includes a readily usable variable indicating whether a respondent supported the government, the opposition, or no party at all in the past election. Figure 14 shows that besides 48 percent who

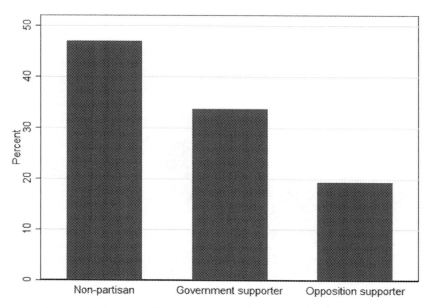

Figure 14 Partisan allegiances in sub-Saharan African countries

are non-partisans, a plurality of 33 percent supported the governing party in the previous election, while 19 percent supported opposition parties.

The Asian Barometer also has a pre-constructed variable capturing whether individuals supported the governing party in the last election (*Q39a*). Figure 15 shows the distribution of individuals across different partisan camps, indicating that half of the respondents in program countries are opposition supporters, 38 percent are government supporters, and 12 percent are non-partisans.

The Latinobarometer is more challenging because it does not include a readily usable measure of partisan alignment but only a forward-looking party choice variable for upcoming elections. Therefore, we construct a measure of *partisan allegiance* by matching the left-right ideological self-placement of a respondent to the partisan orientation of the incumbent. We describe this matching procedure in more detail in the appendix (Table A4). We also replicate this approach for the World Values Survey because it does not include a readily usable measure of partisan alignment either (Table A5). In the Latinobarometer, we can partly enhance the validity of our arguably crude proxy of partisan alignment by requiring individuals to have voted in the past election (*p49stu*). Figure 16 presents the distribution of partisan allegiances in Latin American program countries, showing that about 28 percent of respondents have not voted in the past election, 38 percent share the partisan orientation of the government, and about 34 percent do not share the partisan orientation of the government.

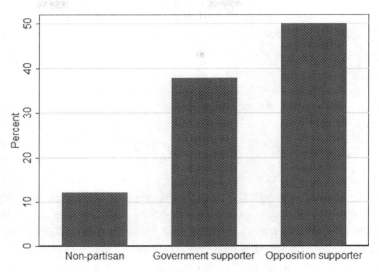

Figure 15 Partisan allegiances in Asian program countries

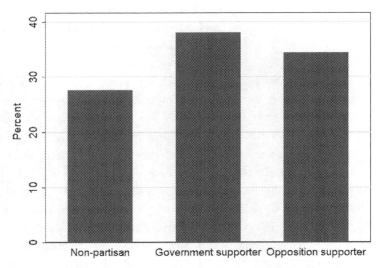

Figure 16 Partisan allegiances in Latin American program countries

3.2.4 Individual-Level Control Variables

In multivariate analyses, we draw on several individual-level control variables, directly available from the surveys. The reason for including these controls is that they could confound the relationship between partisan allegiances and relevant outcomes such as IMF SAP evaluations. Our demographic controls include (logged) age, dummies for whether the respondent is male, lives in an urban area, has a college education, and is unemployed (Almond and Verba 1963; Kaufman and Zuckermann 1998; Pilati 2011; Robertson and Teitelbaum 2011). We also measure political interest, capturing respondents who said they often listen to the news on the radio and who consider themselves as "always interested" in politics. As an objective indicator of political knowledge, we measure whether the respondent recalled the correct name of the finance minister. As to attitudes, beliefs, and values, we use a binary indicator to capture whether the respondent is satisfied with democracy as it is currently practiced in the country. We also measure support for free markets, the public sector, and the privatization of state-owned enterprises. Controlling for these economic values is important to the extent that such values condition evaluations of IMF-sponsored measures. Finally, our most demanding controls gauge respondent evaluations of the state of the economy (Kaufman and Zuckermann 1998). Specifically, we capture whether respondents think the economy is doing worse than twelve months ago and whether they expect it to be deteriorating in the next twelve months. These variables are included to ensure that our results are not driven by individuals who are generally more pessimistic about the economy. For similar reasons, we include a binary variable indicating whether respondents are dissatisfied with the performance of the incumbent. This variable has two important functions. First, it helps us isolate evaluations of the IMF SAP as opposed to evaluations of more general government policies. Second, it proxies the extent to which respondents "like" a particular government – a potential confounder for our analysis because such partisan predispositions could shade their evaluations of IMF SAPs *and* their vote choice in the last election.

To ensure our results are comparable across surveys, we seek to construct sets of control variables that are as similar as possible across the barometers. Perfect congruence is not possible because some questions may not be available or are phrased differently. Nonetheless, we hold that we employ sufficiently similar sets of controls across all surveys to collectively mitigate for the same alternative explanations to our argument. The appendix shows definitions and descriptive statistics for all variables in the Afrobarometer (Table A2), the Asian Barometer (Table A3), the Latinobarometer (Table A4), and the World Values Survey (Table A5).

3.3 Country-Level Data

Our analysis also exploits country-level data on IMF programs and IMF conditionality from the IMF Monitor Database (Kentikelenis, Stubbs, and King 2016). This database is uniquely positioned for our inquiry as it entails

IMF Lending: Partisanship, Punishment, and Protest

information on when a country had an IMF program and how many IMF conditions such programs entailed. The data were obtained from coding Letters of Intent and Memoranda of Economic and Financial Policies – the principal documents which contain the policy conditions governments agree with the IMF for obtaining emergency credit. The data allow us to test two scope conditions of our theoretical argument. First, we expected distributive politics to intensify when a government is under an IMF program. We can test this by examining our individual-level mechanisms for countries under IMF programs and countries not under such programs. Second, we expected that among countries facing IMF adjustment pressures, partisan-based differences in outcomes are greater where governments implement high-discretion programs. These programs are characterized by a greater number of conditions, which provide strategic governments with increased opportunities to lump adjustment burdens onto opposition supporters.

We draw two variables from the IMF Monitor Database. The first is dichotomous and captures whether a country is under an IMF program. The second is a count of the number of conditions that a government faces in a given year. The number of conditions is often taken as a proxy for the overall adjustment burden (Kentikelenis, Stubbs, and King 2016). Following established practice, we consider binding conditions, which include prior actions (measures that countries must implement before being able to draw on IMF loans), quantitative performance criteria (macroeconomic targets for budget balance, inflation rate, and exchange rate, among others), and structural performance criteria (discrete policy instruments that are considered to help countries achieve macroeconomic targets, such as privatizations of state-owned enterprises) (Copelovitch 2010; IMF 2001; Stubbs et al. 2017). These conditions are consequential because governments must fulfill them to avoid delays in the disbursement of IMF credit tranches. As the data are available at the country-year level, we measure both the IMF program dummy and the number of IMF conditions in the year before the survey was taken. This ensures that governments must have attempted to implement at least some conditions, although a contemporaneous effect would also be plausible at least for prior actions that governments will have implemented in the year of loan receipt. Our results are not affected by the choice of lag structure.

In principle, we would also need to think about control variables at the country level because there may be variables that drive both country participation in IMF SAPs and average outcomes of interest such as negative assessments of IMF SAPs and the prevalence of protest. Such variables would include political institutions, macroeconomic fundamentals, and economic policy choices. However, given that there are no repeated observations for countries in the dataset, we can easily account for these country-level characteristics by including

36   *International Relations*

country-fixed effects. With country-fixed effects, we do not need to control for country-specific variables because they will be fully absorbed by the fixed effects.

In our analyses, we always begin with a barebones model with only country-fixed effects, thereby focusing on explaining within-country variation in relevant outcomes across individuals. The rationale for the barebones model is to confront worries about post-treatment bias (Clarke 2005), given that some individual-level variables such as support for markets and perceptions of government performance may themselves be affected by IMF programs. The second set of control variables includes standard demographics as well as attitudes, beliefs, and values that could confound the relationship between partisan allegiances and IMF SAP evaluations. The third set includes variables that help us isolate the variation in IMF-specific evaluations, rather than evaluations of the government more generally, and therefore provides the potentially most stringent test of our argument. We consider the evidence across all sets of control variables to ascertain the robustness of our results.

3.4 Estimation Methods

We use linear probability models because their results are readily interpretable. Moreover, linear probability models easily accommodate country-fixed effects, which is their main advantage over pooled probit-type regressions (Greene 2003). An alternative to fixed-effects regressions would be multi-level random-effect models, which would allow us to include country covariates alongside individual-level variables (Schmidt-Catran and Fairbrother 2016). However, with just a dozen countries in the datasets, the assumption of a normally distributed random intercept is unlikely to hold. Hence, the possibility to control for any unobserved country-level confounders is more important than the efficiency gains from using a multi-level linear model. Our preferred specification, therefore, uses country-fixed effects, and we use multi-level random-intercept models as a robustness check. In the World Values Survey analysis, we further add wave-fixed effects as the longitudinal dataset includes several waves.

To ensure the representativeness of our estimates, we use survey weights, available from the relevant survey datasets. These weights adjust for differences in demographic characteristics within countries and for different population sizes across sample countries.[2] For inference purposes, we compute robust standard errors clustered on countries.[3] Each discussion of our analysis begins with a simple illustrative comparison of our outcome of interest between

---

[2] Variables [afcombwt] in the Afrobarometer, [w_all] in the Asianbarometer, [wt] in the Latinobarometer, and [S017] in the World Values Survey.

[3] Where we have reasons to believe that country-clustered standard errors are misleading due to a low number of clusters, we compute robust standard errors instead.

IMF Lending: Partisanship, Punishment, and Protest 37

government and opposition supporters. We then proceed to examine if the differences found between these groups remain significant in multivariate analysis.

4 How IMF Programs Affect Distributive Politics

In this section, we examine how partisan allegiances shape individual experiences and perceptions of IMF SAPs. We briefly remind the reader that our core theoretical arguments lead us to expect that distributive politics will intensify when countries go under IMF SAPs. Governments typically must cut expenditures and undergo painful reforms when they agree on adjustment programs with the IMF. We expect governments to seek political advantage even when implementing painful reforms. In these cases, we think that governments who wish to maintain their winning coalition and retain political power will allocate adjustment burdens onto opposition supporters while shielding their supporters as much as possible. They will protect or reward their supporters utilizing the discretion that is afforded to them as part of IMF reform programs while meeting many of the conditions agreed upon with the IMF. We anticipate governments utilizing the privatization of state assets to benefit their supporters. When these programs permit spending on infrastructure, we expect that to occur in the regions that supported them. Finally, when governments must retrench public-sector workers, we expect them to find creative ways to burden opposition supporters with the costs of reductions in the size of the public-sector. We begin with an illustrative case study of Ghana. We then provide econometric tests of our arguments first presenting results from Afrobarometer, followed by complementary evidence from Asian Barometer and Latinobarometer.

4.1 Case-Study Evidence on the Distributional Politics of Adjustment

Our intertemporal case study of Ghana provides an example of our proposed mechanisms.[4] Our subsequent large-N analysis suggests that Ghana reflects an average case from the Afrobarometer sample, given that similar patterns of diverging IMF SAP evaluations and partisan politics occur in Malawi, Tanzania, and Zambia. A case-study approach allows us to overcome a key limitation of the survey data: they only represent a snapshot in time. Drawing on a rich body of literature on Ghanaian politics (Abdulai and Hickey 2016; Appiah-Kubi 2001; Brierley 2021; Handley 2007; Harding 2015; Ninsin 1998; Youde 2005), we exploit intertemporal variation in the Ghanaian case due to

---

[4] Some of the case material in this section is based on a journal article we published in the *Review of International Political Economy.*

38 *International Relations*

a change in government while the country was under IMF assistance. This allows us to demonstrate how the allocation of adjustment burdens across different societal groups changes as the party controlling the government changes.

While Ghana's Enhanced Structural Adjustment Facility Policy Framework Paper (IMF 1999) laid out a broad range of financial and structural reforms, including for example divestiture of state-owned enterprises and infrastructure projects, the government retained discretion in how to meet these targets. We find that both the Rawlings government and the subsequent Kufuor administration tried to use IMF funding to protect their own supporters. Rawlings advantaged party elites in the privatization and liberalization process while rolling out a social support package that disproportionately benefited his supporters. Kufuor, who had his support base among local entrepreneurs, implemented a raft of pro-business reforms and regional infrastructure projects to reward long-standing areas of support and swing states which helped him gain office.

With the backing of the IMF, Rawlings turned the state-controlled economy established under Kwame Nkrumah into a liberal market economy, involving the privatization of state-owned enterprises and the liberalization of the Ghanaian economy to foreign investors. These reforms *continued* with the Kufuor administration who submitted the country under the Heavily Indebted Poor Countries (HIPC) initiative, which linked debt relief to further conditionality. From this perspective, both administrations complied with the IMF's reform agenda, while having different support bases.[5]

4.1.1 Adjustment Policies of the Rawlings Administration

For two decades, Ghana was ruled by Jerry Rawlings, first as military chief (1981–93) and then as the elected leader of the National Democratic Congress (NDC) (1993–2001). Rawlings took power on December 31, 1981, in the fifth coup that had taken place in thirty-five years, and began a near consecutive series of agreements with the IMF in 1983 (Akonor 2013). Facing re-election for the first time in 1996, Rawlings asserted himself through distributive politics. He targeted rural areas with capital spending on roads, rather than cutting capital spending as agreed upon with the IMF, with a total expenditure 20 percent higher than the government had originally budgeted (Akonor 2013, 99–101). Ninsin (1998, 226–27) astutely observes how Rawlings used the state to reward would-be supporters with the distribution of limited national resources:

---

[5] The IMF's Monitoring of Fund Arrangements (MONA) database shows that Ghana met all quantitative targets in its 1995 ESAF program. While the IMF transitioned to a new system for collecting information during 1999–2003, we lack implementation records for the 1999 ESAF program. However, other IMF reports indicate that the Ghanaian government was highly committed to implement program targets (IMF 1998, 1999, 2000).

IMF Lending: Partisanship, Punishment, and Protest

> Rawlings and his party men won the 1996 elections because the electorate perceived them as the ones who control the scarce resources needed for development of their communities. They were also the ones with demonstrable capacity and commitment to deliver or punish communities that do not show sufficient support at the polls.

Both ethnicity and anticipated material benefits prompted voters to support the winning party (Abdulai and Hickey 2016; Youde 2005). The president used his executive authority to appoint teachers across the country for political advantage. Citizens rewarded these appointments in presidential elections with larger shares of votes for the incumbent (Harding 2015). Drawing on international aid, Rawlings successfully used electrification to both reward supporters and bring new voters into the fold as NDC voting increased in constituencies that received electrification (Briggs 2012, 603).

Privileging Party Elites in the Privatization Process

Rawlings began privatizing a range of state-owned enterprises (SOEs) as part of an IMF adjustment program agreed upon in 1986 (Akonor 2013, 87). He utilized the IMF-mandated divestiture process – the transfer of public assets into private hands – for political gain, through a variety of questionable practices (Appiah-Kubi 2001). For example, the Divestiture Implementation Committee (DIC), the government agency created to handle the process, never publicized the initial divestiture transactions – interested parties were simply requested to contact the DIC or the relevant sector ministry. Appiah-Kubi (2001, 224) notes that this lack of transparency led to "widespread allegations of opportunistic behavior by bureaucrats and top government executives eager to cream off sizeable rents from their control of SOEs."

The period 1989–1999 saw over 70 percent of Ghana's SOEs privatized (Appiah-Kubi 2001, 211). Between 1991 and 1998, divestiture receipts on average accounted for 8.5 percent of total government revenue (Appiah-Kubi 2001, 216). While this revenue steadied the Ghanaian economy, it also allowed the government to stabilize taxes and helped Rawlings maintain partisan support. As Appiah-Kubi (2001, 217) describes, the forgoing of tax increases provided a "congenial sociopolitical atmosphere that paved the way for the smooth transition from military rule to democratic multi-party governance."

Privatization and the Maintenance of Public-Sector Salaries

Privatizing SOEs not only provided a significant source of revenue for the government during the 1990s but also increased employment rates and wages in previously moribund SOEs (Appiah-Kubi 2001, 214). The Rawlings administration used its control over the public sector to reward those working in it, despite being under pressure from the IMF to bring tax receipts and spending closer into balance. In the spring of 2000, amid an IMF program, the Rawlings government announced via the state radio a "20-percent across-the-board salary hike for civil servants, teachers, nurses and members of the judiciary" (The New Humanitarian 2000). This did not go unnoticed by the IMF. In late May 2000, the IMF representative to Ghana, Girma Bergashaw said to Reuters he was "uncomfortable with [the] 20% wage increase announced this week by the government for some categories of public sector workers" (GhanaWeb 2000). These sizable salary increases dovetailed with other policies promoted by the Rawlings administration which sought to privilege public-sector workers and provides some evidence that the government sought to protect particular groups from the burdens of adjustment.

Support Packages and the Protection of Particular Groups from the Burdens of IMF Adjustment

The Program of Action to Mitigate the Social Costs of Adjustment (PAMSCAD) developed by the Ghanaian health and education ministries, in conjunction with the World Bank and UNICEF, came about in response to the negative socioeconomic consequences of the IMF agreements that began in 1983 (Reddy 1998). PAMSCAD was designed to maintain political support for the government (Jeong 1995). In unusually blunt language, the World Bank noted the politics of this support: "While these actions may not translate into direct support for adjustment per se, they may foster confidence in the government at a critical time" (Marc et al. 1995, 35). Notwithstanding the debate about the effectiveness of the PAMSCAD in ameliorating the negative consequences of conditionality (Boafo-Arthur 1999; Jeong 1995; Marc et al. 1995), it was designed to cushion government supporters from these burdens. It provided widespread support for a range of sectors which the government relied upon for support (Marc et al. 1995, 103–6).

In contrast with their active involvement in the design, implementation, and compliance with IMF program lending, the Rawlings administration displayed little effort to mediate the negative domestic effects of the IMF and other Western powers selling gold on the international market. The gold sale would have detrimental economic consequences in the Ashanti area of the country, a hotbed of opposition support. The Rawlings administration muted reaction indicated that saving the jobs of individuals who mostly voted for the opposition was not a government priority. Beyond expressing "concern" about the IMF's decision (GhanaWeb 1999a), the government did little to stop the sale from taking place even though the Ashanti Goldfields Company (AGC) indicated that

IMF Lending: Partisanship, Punishment, and Protest 41

2,000 workers may have to be laid off as a result of the slump in gold prices (GhanaWeb 1999b). In her detailed account of the affair, Handley (2007) notes how President Rawlings had also developed a personal animosity toward the AGC CEO Sam Jonah, because of his criticism of the President. Rawlings regarded Jonah as a threat to his power; this animosity spilled over into the political choice to not support the Ashanti Gold Company to weaken its CEO and thereby see off his potential threat. Not surprisingly the region overwhelmingly favored the opposition in the December 2000 election (Anebo 2001, 83).

4.1.2 Ghanaian Adjustment Politics under the Kufuor Administration

On January 7, 2001, Rawlings's nominee, vice-president, John Atta Mills, lost the NDC's bid to retain power losing to the opposition leader John Agyekum Kufuor from the New Patriotic Party (NPP). The NPP was strongly tied to the indigenous entrepreneurial elite, a group that suffered under Rawlings (GhanaWeb 2001c; Handley 2007). The new Kufuor administration continued its engagement with the IMF. Facing dire economic circumstances, Kufuor instructed his administration to adopt the HIPC initiative to unlock debt relief and free up fiscal space. The initiative reduced Ghana's debt overhang to facilitate investment into the domestic economy. The new administration enacted many adjustment reforms to promote the business sectors of the economy, which favored Kufuor's entrepreneurial base, while at the same time ignoring the demands of civil society organizations (Crawford and Abdulai 2009, 102–3). This is illustrated by a union leader who complained about the spending cuts proposed by the Kufuor administration:

> Mr Chigabatia expressed regret that workers have been left out in the debate on the economy even though the decisions taken affect them directly. He said workers are tired of the countless reform and economic packages fashioned by the World Bank and IMF, adding, "none of these things has served the interest of workers." . . . Mr Chigabatia said issues such as salaries should not be put in the budget as they have the tendency of putting undue pressure on workers. (GhanaWeb 2001a)

There is also evidence that the Kufuor administration directed infrastructure projects to regions of the country that supported his election. As part of the new lending by the IMF and the World Bank, Kufuor's administration received a total of $462 million to support Ghana's developmental projects (GhanaWeb 2001b). Part of this package contained "$220 million . . . for road projects, notably Accra-Kumasi and Accra-Cape Coast dual carriage roads" (GhanaWeb 2001b). Kumasi is the capital of the Ashanti region, and the region which provided Kufuor with the highest percentage of support, totaling 80.5 percent of the vote in the presidential run-off increasing from 65.8 percent of the vote in 1996 (PeaceFMOnline 1996a). While Cape Coast was also one of the largest supporters for Kufuor, it also represented an important swing region moving from 43.0 percent support for Kufuor in the 1996 election to 60.2 percent of the vote in the presidential run-off in 2000 (PeaceFMOnline 1996b). Kufuor appears to reward both his support base in the Ashanti region as well as thanking the newly supportive region of the Cape Coast with substantial infrastructure investment. The behavior of the Kufuor administration ties in with research on Ghana where voters can attribute the provision of a particular good (roads) to a particular politician, they will reward those politicians with their votes (Harding 2015).

Our illustrative case of Ghana provides us with some evidence that governments may utilize the flexibility given to them in complying with IMF mandates to advantage their partisans and place the burdens of adjustment disproportionately on supporters of the opposition. We found that such patterns of distributional politics are particularly salient where governments have direct control over policy implementation, notably for public-sector employment, public infrastructure, and the divestiture process. To probe the plausibility of these findings beyond the case of Ghana, we now turn to our large-N analysis using survey data.

4.2 Survey Research on Sub-Saharan Africa

4.2.1 Research Design

We use a sample of 21,531 respondents in twelve sub-Saharan African countries from the first wave of Afrobarometer (1999–2001). Our effective sample is smaller due to the omission of countries in which relevant questions were not asked, or individuals for whom the question is not relevant because they are unaware of the IMF SAP. Our main dependent variable draws on the Afrobarometer survey question asking people about the pocketbook effects of the IMF SAP of their country, measured on a five-point Likert scale. For our analysis, we create the dichotomous variable SAP MADE MY LIFE WORSE by combining the two response categories for deteriorating life circumstances.

Our main independent variable is based on whether the individual is a supporter of the governing party, a supporter of an opposition party, or not a supporter of any party at all. It is available from the survey, constructed by comparing the incumbent party and the party identification variable in the survey dataset. As our argument builds on differences in partisan allegiances, we drop the neutral category in our main analysis and construct the binary indicator OPPOSITION SUPPORTER. This allows us to directly compare pocketbook evaluations between opposition supporters and government supporters. In robustness tests, we use a trichotomous variable comparing government supporters (supporter of the winning party), opposition supporters (supporter of the losing party), and the neutral category (those who do not support any party).

Independent variables at the country level include a dummy for whether the country has been under an IMF program in the year before the survey, as well as the total number of IMF conditions in that year. We draw both pieces of information from the IMF Monitor Database. Using these variables allows us to examine whether distributive politics intensifies in the presence of IMF SAPs, especially when such programs leave governments with greater potential for distributive politics by including more adjustment burdens. We therefore expect partisan-driven differences in IMF SAP evaluations to be bigger where the country has an IMF program, and the government faces a greater number of binding policy conditions.

For control variables, we focus on individual-level controls because country-fixed effects already account for the confounding impact of country-level variables on our outcomes. While our first set of controls only includes these fixed effects, the second set includes individual-level demographic characteristics and respondent values, as described earlier. The third set of controls, which were also described in the previous section adds variables capturing respondent evaluations of the government more generally.

A final consideration pertains to the choice of respondent sample. Here we need to consider that people who have not heard about the IMF SAP do not record any perceptions about it. The sample therefore only includes respondents who have heard about the SAP in their country. We may be concerned that people who heard about the SAP are different from people who have not heard about it and that this difference is related to partisanship and potentially other unobserved respondent characteristics. As this selection process could induce bias into our estimates, we also estimate a two-stage model in which we jointly estimate the determinants of respondent awareness about the IMF SAP and program evaluations for those being aware. The two-stage model is necessary only if unobserved factors are driving both IMF SAP awareness and IMF SAP evaluations. Reassuringly, the main results are not affected by either modeling alternative.

4.2.2 Illustrative Evidence

We now present illustrative evidence for our argument from the Afrobarometer sample. Figure 17 provides suggestive support for the argument that negative

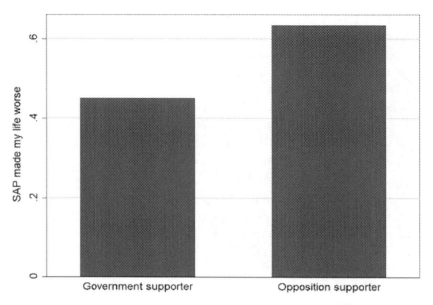

Figure 17 Partisan allegiances and IMF SAP pocketbook evaluations

evaluations of IMF SAPs are more prevalent among opposition supporters. While 45.1 percent (95% CI: 43.1–47.7%) of government supporters consider that the IMF SAP made their life worse, the corresponding figure is 63.5 percent (95% CI: 60.8–66.2%) for opposition supporters. A t-test finds the difference of 18.4 percentage points to be statistically significant (p<0.001).

Figure 18 probes the notion that the scope for distributive politics – and therefore the partisan-based differences in IMF SAP evaluations – should be larger where countries are under an IMF program. Indeed, we find a similar prevalence of negative pocketbook evaluations of IMF SAPs between government supporters and opposition supporters in countries that were not under an IMF program. A t-test confirms that the 2.4 percentage-point difference in outcomes is not statistically significant. In contrast, where countries are under an IMF program, partisan-based differences are large: For about 42.3 percent (95% CI: 40.1–44.9%) of government supporters, IMF SAPs have made their lives worse, compared to about 64.5 percent (95% CI: 61.6–67.5%) for opposition supporters. The difference of 22.2 percentage points is statistically significant (p<0.001).

Finally, we exploit differences in IMF program design across countries. Figure 19 shows that there is no discernible partisan difference in pocketbook evaluations for IMF SAPs with different numbers of conditions. We will scrutinize this finding again after controlling for observable confounders.

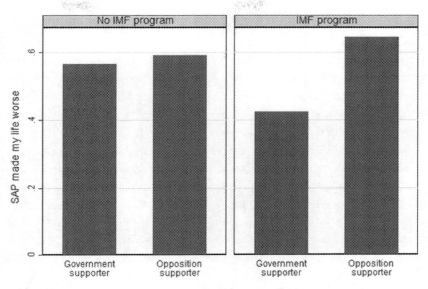

Figure 18 Partisan allegiances, IMF program exposure, and IMF SAP pocketbook evaluations

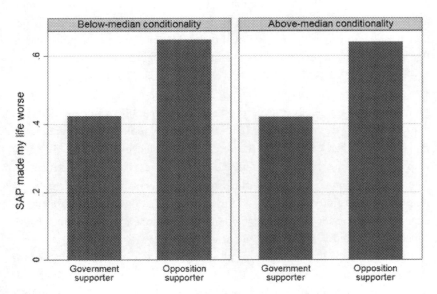

Figure 19 Partisan allegiances, IMF program design, and IMF SAP pocketbook evaluations

46 *International Relations*

4.2.3 Regression Results

Table 1 shows the relationship between partisan allegiances and whether respondents think that the IMF SAP made their life worse. Our key quantity of interest is the coefficient for opposition supporters, which indicates the percentage-point difference in the prevalence of a negative pocketbook evaluation of the IMF SAP compared to government supporters. Different columns show models with three different sets of control variables.

Our results provide evidence for our first hypothesis that partisan supporters of the opposition view the consequences of IMF program lending more negatively than partisans who support the government. We find that opposition supporters have a significantly higher likelihood of a negative pocketbook evaluation of the IMF SAP, compared to government supporters ($p<0.05$). For example, in the last model, opposition supporters have a likelihood of 64.3 percent (95% CI: 50.3–78.3%) of a negative pocketbook evaluation compared to 52.2 percent (95% CI: 32.5–71.9%) for government supporters.

Coefficient estimates of control variables are consistent with theoretical expectations. Among the respondents who have heard about the IMF SAP, older people tend to be unhappier with SAPs. A similar finding emerges for unemployed people. Urban residents are less likely to have a negative IMF SAP evaluation. We also find evidence that political interest and radio consumption are negatively related to pocketbook evaluations, while politically knowledgeable people are generally more critical of IMF SAPs. There is some evidence that people who prefer capitalism and support privatization view the pocketbook effects of IMF SAPs more negatively. In the models with extended control variables, we find that individuals with generally more pessimistic evaluations of the economy and notably the performance of the incumbent are more likely to express negative evaluations of IMF SAPs. This may look surprising at first but makes sense when considering the role of unfulfilled expectations for these respondents. None of the remaining controls reaches statistical significance. The fact that our core result is consistent across the three specifications is reassuring, especially when considering that evaluations of the state of the economy and the level of dissatisfaction with incumbent performance absorb substantive variation in the outcome of interest.

Table 2 presents the results from split-sample models in which we allow for the partisan-induced difference in IMF SAP evaluations to vary by whether or not countries are under an IMF SAP. We find that in countries with IMF programs, 45.0 percent (95% CI: 15.3–74.7%) of government supporters and 64.8 percent (95% CI: 40.1–89.6%) of opposition supporters have negative pocketbook evaluations of IMF SAPs. As the confidence intervals of effects for

Table 1 Partisan allegiance and pocketbook evaluation in the Afrobarometer sample

	(1)		(2)		(3)	
Opposition supporter	0.153*	(0.070)	0.155**	(0.061)	0.121**	(0.047)
Male			0.031	(0.022)	0.028	(0.022)
(Logged) age			0.074**	(0.025)	0.068**	(0.024)
Urban			−0.047*	(0.021)	−0.047*	(0.023)
Unemployed			0.076**	(0.026)	0.068**	(0.024)
Educated			−0.041	(0.023)	−0.041	(0.022)
Radio listener			−0.024*	(0.013)	−0.025*	(0.013)
Politically interested			−0.047***	(0.010)	−0.040***	(0.009)
Politically knowledgeable			0.088***	(0.014)	0.090***	(0.014)
Satisfied with democracy			−0.007	(0.026)	0.006	(0.025)
Prefers free market			0.007	(0.029)	0.007	(0.031)
Supports capitalism			0.034***	(0.009)	0.033***	(0.009)
Supports public sector			0.017	(0.010)	0.014	(0.010)
Supports privatization			0.091**	(0.038)	0.091**	(0.036)
Worse now than 12 months ago					0.055***	(0.013)
Worse in 12 months					0.071**	(0.030)
Dissatisfied with president					0.160**	(0.063)
Observations	3679		3641		3641	
Adjusted R2	0.183		0.206		0.219	

Notes: Dependent variable is SAP MADE MY LIFE WORSE. Sample includes only respondents who are aware of the IMF SAP. Linear probability model with survey weights, country-fixed effects, and country-clustered standard errors. Significance levels: * p<.1 ** p<.05 *** p<.01

Table 2 Partisan allegiances, IMF program exposure, and pocketbook evaluations in the Afrobarometer sample

	Current IMF program			No current IMF program		
	(1)	(2)	(3)	(4)	(5)	(6)
Opposition supporter	0.263*** (0.065)	0.250*** (0.057)	0.198*** (0.045)	0.022 (0.022)	0.032 (0.016)	0.028 (0.018)
Male		0.001 (0.025)	−0.004 (0.024)		0.072* (0.006)	0.073* (0.010)
(Logged) age		0.094** (0.037)	0.083* (0.035)		0.056* (0.007)	0.052* (0.006)
Urban		−0.032 (0.026)	−0.031 (0.027)		−0.080 (0.030)	−0.083 (0.030)
Unemployed		0.049 (0.060)	0.043 (0.055)		0.092* (0.015)	0.084 (0.013)
Educated		−0.016 (0.030)	−0.019 (0.030)		−0.070* (0.006)	−0.067* (0.010)
Radio listener		−0.017 (0.022)	−0.021 (0.023)		−0.016 (0.004)	−0.015** (0.001)
Politically interested		−0.046** (0.016)	−0.042** (0.016)		−0.035 (0.021)	−0.030 (0.013)
Politically knowledgeable		0.076** (0.022)	0.079** (0.022)		0.085* (0.008)	0.086 (0.017)
Satisfied with democracy		−0.042** (0.015)	−0.023 (0.017)		0.044 (0.025)	0.042 (0.026)
Prefers free market		−0.026 (0.020)	−0.029 (0.020)		0.064 (0.025)	0.065 (0.028)
Supports capitalism		0.032 (0.019)	0.034 (0.019)		0.030*** (0.000)	0.030* (0.003)
Supports public sector		−0.005 (0.017)	−0.005 (0.019)		0.012 (0.019)	0.011 (0.025)
Supports privatization		0.106 (0.057)	0.101 (0.056)		0.058 (0.036)	0.061 (0.031)
Worse now than 12 months ago			0.062** (0.019)			0.051 (0.027)
Worse now than in 12 months			0.045 (0.024)			0.198* (0.018)
Dissatisfied with president			0.161*** (0.034)			−0.104 (0.025)
Observations	2964	2926	2926	715	715	715
Adjusted R2	0.208	0.229	0.245	0.158	0.180	0.187

Notes: Dependent variable is SAP made my life worse. Sample includes only respondents who are aware of the IMF SAP. Linear probability model with survey weights, country-fixed effects, and country-clustered standard errors. Significance levels: * p<.1 ** p<.05 *** p<.01

IMF Lending: Partisanship, Punishment, and Protest

each partisan group do not include the point prediction of the other group, the difference is statistically significant. In countries without IMF program exposure, this difference becomes insignificant – here 60.9 percent of government supporters and 64.7 of the opposition supporters have negative pocketbook evaluations of IMF SAPs. This suggests that IMF program participation intensifies distributive politics and thus increases the observable partisan difference in IMF SAP pocketbook evaluations.

4.2.4 Threats to Inference, Robustness Tests, and Further Analyses

One objection to our results so far is that governments may not be able to identify different partisans, which would limit the extent of distributional politics. We argue that the scope of distributive politics may indeed be limited to sectors in which the government has direct control over the allocation of resources, such as employment contracts in the public sector. Hence, individuals who are in public-sector employment and support the opposition view the consequences of IMF program lending more negatively than those who are not. The results corroborate our expectations. While different partisans differ in their IMF SAP evaluations, effect magnitudes are consistently larger among public-sector workers compared to workers in other sectors ($p<0.01$) (Table A6).

Another objection to our results is that different IMF SAP evaluations are driven purely by perceptions. Different partisans may be inclined to interpret their experience with the IMF SAP differently, regardless of actual differences in their treatment by the government. To allay such concerns, we exploit an index of objective hardship, constructed from a battery of Afrobarometer questions. These questions capture the frequency with which respondents have gone without food, health care, potable water, and income. For example, the food deprivation question reads: "In the last twelve months, how often have you or your family: gone without enough food to eat?" Answer categories for all questions include "never," "rarely," "sometimes," "often," and non-responses. We create an index DEPRIVATION by adding responses from all four items (where "never" is 0, "rarely" is 1, "sometimes" is 2, and "often" is 3). The empirical range is from zero to twelve. Because the survey question is not specifically about deprivation *induced by* the IMF SAP, we need to leverage additional macro-level variation in IMF program participation and IMF program design to identify the effect of distributive politics in the context of the IMF SAP.

Our results provide strong support for the notion that partisan-based differences in IMF SAP pocketbook evaluations are not simply driven by perceptions but objective hardships. Compared to countries without IMF program experience, being an opposition supporter is significantly related to deprivation in countries under an IMF program (Table A7). Comparing across programs with different designs, we obtain less significant patterns, although the direction of the effect is indicative: In a high-conditionality scenario, being an opposition supporter tends to be related to more deprivation than being a government supporter, and compared to a low-conditionality scenario (Table A8).

Table 3 shows the results of split-sample models in which we allow for the partisan-induced difference in IMF SAP evaluations to vary by the number of IMF conditions. Here we only consider countries with IMF programs and split the sample at the median number of conditions. Consistent with our argument that more conditions imply a greater potential for governments to allocate burdens along partisan lines, we find a significant relationship between partisan allegiances and IMF SAP evaluations only in the high-conditionality case, but not in the low-conditionality case. In the former case, we find at least a 10.6 percentage-point difference in IMF SAP evaluations ($p<0.05$) – with 30.5 percent for government supporters and 41.1 percent for opposition supporters. In the latter case, we find a 10.4 percentage-point difference that is not statistically significant.

We have so far only included respondents who have heard about the IMF program. This could induce selection bias into our results to the extent that unobserved respondent characteristics that correlate with partisanship drive both their interest in the IMF SAP and their related pocketbook evaluation. To mitigate this bias, we perform a two-stage selection model in which we first predict whether respondents heard about the IMF program, before examining the determinants of a negative pocketbook evaluation among aware individuals. We predict awareness about the IMF SAP with two binary variables that are unlikely to directly affect IMF SAP evaluations. The first is political interest – whether respondents consider themselves interested in politics. The second is objective knowledge about politics, specifically whether a respondent correctly recalled the name of the finance minister. Both variables are available from the survey. We find significant partisan differences in IMF SAP evaluations, even considering that incumbent supporters tend to be more aware of IMF SAPs (Table A9). When comparing across IMF SAPs, we also find that as a government faces more conditions, the partisan difference concerning negative IMF SAP evaluations widens (Table A10).

Some have argued that politics in an African context is organized along both ethnic and partisan lines (Bratton, Bhavnani, and Chen 2012). From a methodological point of view, a related critique is that political allegiances may change quickly and thus become endogenous to distributional outcomes. Probing whether our results also hold for ethnicity, therefore, holds promise to strengthen our inferences. We would expect that individuals belonging to an

Table 3 Partisan allegiances, IMF conditionality, and pocketbook evaluations in the Afrobarometer sample

	Above-median conditionality						Below-median conditionality					
	(1)		(2)		(3)		(4)		(5)		(6)	
Opposition supporter	0.146***	(0.014)	0.121***	(0.016)	0.106**	(0.025)	0.154	(0.069)	0.137	(0.074)	0.104	(0.047)
Male			0.027	(0.024)	0.024	(0.024)			0.033	(0.012)	0.033*	(0.011)
(Logged) age			0.051	(0.028)	0.050	(0.029)			0.054	(0.040)	0.054	(0.037)
Urban			0.024	(0.028)	0.025	(0.029)			−0.030	(0.016)	−0.028	(0.018)
Unemployed			−0.056	(0.031)	−0.057	(0.031)			−0.013	(0.017)	−0.019	(0.019)
Educated			−0.026	(0.039)	−0.026	(0.039)			0.092*	(0.025)	0.090*	(0.024)
Radio listener			−0.003	(0.019)	−0.005	(0.018)			−0.032	(0.012)	−0.030	(0.011)
Politically interested			0.035	(0.017)	0.037	(0.016)			0.011	(0.014)	0.012	(0.013)
Politically knowledgeable			0.160***	(0.012)	0.159***	(0.013)			0.104**	(0.013)	0.104**	(0.011)
Satisfied with democracy			−0.018	(0.008)	−0.009	(0.010)			0.005	(0.010)	0.013	(0.008)
Prefers free market			0.024	(0.017)	0.024	(0.016)			0.021	(0.012)	0.019	(0.010)
Supports capitalism			0.034	(0.019)	0.036	(0.018)			0.017	(0.025)	0.017	(0.026)
Supports public sector			−0.005	(0.007)	−0.001	(0.008)			0.012	(0.039)	0.010	(0.039)
Supports privatization			0.048	(0.067)	0.046	(0.067)			0.014	(0.042)	0.013	(0.040)
Worse now than 12 months ago					0.021	(0.027)					0.013*	(0.004)
Worse now than in 12 months					0.031	(0.034)					0.023*	(0.006)
Dissatisfied with president					0.103	(0.049)					0.075	(0.055)
Observations	2806		2769		2769		3889		3780		3780	
Adjusted R2	0.226		0.261		0.266		0.082		0.126		0.131	

Notes: Dependent variable is SAP made my life worse. Sample includes only respondents who are aware of the IMF SAP and only countries with an ongoing IMF program. Linear probability model with survey weights, country-fixed effects, and country-clustered standard errors. Significance levels: * p<.1 ** p<.05 *** p<.01

ethnically discriminated group will have less favorable evaluations of the IMF SAP than members of a powerful group. We rely on group status information from the Ethnic Power Relations dataset (Vogt et al. 2015). The remaining challenge is to identify to which ethnic group a respondent belongs, which is not directly available from the Afrobarometer. From the Afrobarometer, we identify the main language that respondents speak. In some cases, it is possible to infer the ethnic group from the language spoken. Our focus is to distinguish groups that control the government from those that are powerless – if not entirely discriminated against. We disregard groups that have junior-partner status in the government. Our relevant comparisons are thus between powerful groups and powerless groups. Where such ascriptions are not possible, for example, because ethnicity is not politically relevant, we exclude respondents of such countries. Our remaining sample has 6,136 individuals from five countries, of which 5,760 individuals are members of the powerful group and 376 individuals are from powerless groups. The sample further reduces when requiring that individuals must have heard about the SAP in their country.

Replicating our main results with markers of ethnicity, we find a significantly higher likelihood of negative pocketbook evaluations of IMF SAPs among members of powerless ethnic groups, compared to members of powerful groups (Table A11). Specifically, being a member of an ethnically powerless group increases the likelihood of a negative pocketbook evaluation by about 14.7 percent (95% CI: 8.9–20.5%), relative to being a member of an ethnically powerful group. In further analysis, we find a wider ethnicity gap in pocketbook evaluations between IMF program countries and non-program countries (Table A12). The effect of being a member of an ethnic minority on a negative pocketbook evaluation is amplified by an additional ten percentage points (95% CI: 7.9–11.1%) if a country has an active IMF program.[6]

Finally, we probe the robustness of our findings to alternative econometric modeling choices. We re-run our models using survey-adjusted probit regressions. Our results are qualitatively similar, showing a statistically significant difference in IMF SAP evaluations across partisan groups (Table A13). Partisan differences are significantly larger when the country is under an IMF program (Table A14) and when the government faces more IMF conditions (Table A15). In addition, our results hold for random-intercept multi-level models. While we are careful not to over-interpret the findings given the small number of country clusters (Stegmueller 2013), we corroborate the statistically significant difference in IMF SAP evaluations across partisan groups (Table A16), which grows

---

[6] Due to limited observations on ethnicity in program countries, we cannot estimate ethnicity-based evaluation gaps across different programs.

IMF Lending: Partisanship, Punishment, and Protest

even larger when conditioning on IMF program participation (Table A17) and the number of IMF conditions (Table A18).

4.3 Survey Research on Asia

To probe the generalizability of our findings beyond sub-Saharan Africa, we draw on the second wave of the Asian Barometer from 2005–2008. This survey wave is the only one that includes questions on IMF confidence, government bias, and protest, besides a partisanship variable, which offers a unique opportunity to study attitudes toward both the IMF and the government. Since the questions are not worded specifically about IMF SAPs, we identify the effects of distributive politics under IMF SAPs through a country-level interaction term with IMF program participation. Countries with IMF program experience in the Asian Barometer include Indonesia, Mongolia, and Vietnam. Within this group of countries, we also examine distributive politics under different program designs in terms of the number of IMF conditions.

We use two dependent variables. The first is GOVERNMENT BIAS – a binary variable capturing whether a respondent somewhat disagrees or strongly disagrees with the statement that "the government treats people equally", measured on a five-point Likert scale with a neutral category. The second is BAD IMPRESSION OF THE IMF, derived from a survey question asking respondents to rate their impression of the IMF on a scale from 1 to 10, where 1 is the worst and 10 is the best and where we consider a rating of at most 3 out of 10 as bad.

The main predictors are measured at two levels. At the individual level, we include OPPOSITION SUPPORTER, a binary variable that indicates whether the individual supported opposition parties in the past election, rather than the government party, and which is missing otherwise. At the country level, we include a fractional indicator capturing the time a country has been under an IMF program in the past three years. We deviate from our previous measurement here because there would otherwise be no country with IMF exposure. For the same reason, we average the number of binding CONDITIONS over the three years before the survey year. While using three-year averages is an empirically motivated choice related to the low incidence of IMF SAPs in Asia, this choice is conceptually meaningful because the typical IMF program lasts about three years.

In choosing our control variables, we try to match our specification from Afrobarometer. We construct three sets of controls, beginning with country-fixed effects, subsequently adding demographic variables and values and beliefs, as well as attitudes and evaluations. Demographic characteristics include male, age, urban, employment, and years of education; values and beliefs entail support for democracy and support for the market economy. Our most demanding specification adds indicators for whether respondents perceive the economy as being worse now than twelve months ago, the extent to which respondents think the government should be obeyed, and support for majority decisions. The appendix presents variable definitions and descriptive statistics for all variables (Table A3).

After presenting illustrative evidence and bivariate t-tests, we perform linear probability models with country-fixed effects and survey weights. We cluster standard errors on the country. Testing our argument requires including a cross-level interaction between the number of conditions and the partisan allegiance of an individual. This assumes that more conditions engender greater potential for allocation adjustment burdens, which biased governments will lump on the opposition.

4.3.1 Illustrative Evidence

Figure 20 shows the perceived biasedness of the government for different partisan groups and across Asian program countries with different conditionality. Several observations stand out. First, we find that more people think their government is biased in countries with high-conditionality programs compared to those with low-conditionality programs. Second, in the high-conditionality scenario, opposition supporters are significantly more likely than government

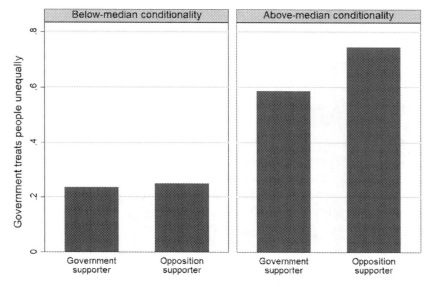

Figure 20 Partisan allegiance, IMF conditionality, and government bias

supporters to assess the government as biased. A t-test confirms the difference of 14.1 percentage points as statistically significant (p<0.001). This is not the case in the low-conditionality scenario, where the difference is just 1.2 percentage points and not significant (p=0.63). Both pieces of evidence are in line with our argument that more conditions provide governments with additional burdens to allocate, notably upon opposition supporters.

Figure 21 replicates this analysis concerning the prevalence of a bad impression of the IMF as the outcome variable. Interestingly, we obtain qualitatively different response patterns. In the high-conditionality scenario, government supporters are more likely to dislike the IMF than opposition supporters, while the reverse holds in the low-conditionality scenario. A plausible interpretation of these findings is that people are capable of correctly attributing responsibility for their fortunes. Opposition supporters do not seem to blame the IMF when governments implement high-discretion programs with many conditions, but may attribute blame to the government.

4.3.2 Regression Results

Table 4 examines the relationship between partisan allegiance, IMF program exposure, and (the perception of) government bias under various sets of control variables. We find a statistically significant positive interaction between

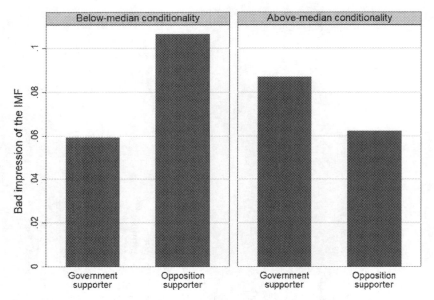

Figure 21 Partisan allegiance, IMF conditionality, and bad impression of the IMF

Table 4 Partisan allegiances, IMF program exposure, and government bias in Asia

	(1)		(2)		(3)	
IMF program	−0.696***	(0.082)	−0.667***	(0.084)	−0.690***	(0.082)
Opposition supporter	0.043***	(0.015)	0.048***	(0.016)	0.037**	(0.016)
(Interaction)	0.097***	(0.035)	0.077**	(0.036)	0.074**	(0.036)
Male			0.009	(0.012)	0.011	(0.012)
(Logged) age			−0.036***	(0.010)	−0.034***	(0.009)
Urban			−0.024**	(0.012)	−0.016	(0.012)
Employed			0.053***	(0.017)	0.049***	(0.017)
Education			−0.027***	(0.008)	−0.024***	(0.008)
Supports democracy			0.010	(0.012)	0.020*	(0.012)
Democracy over growth			−0.001	(0.016)	0.001	(0.016)
Economy got worse					0.095***	(0.017)
Must obey government					−0.111***	(0.013)
Supports majority rule					−0.013	(0.013)
Observations	8489		7050		7050	
Adjusted R2	0.222		0.182		0.199	

Notes: Dependent variable is government bias. Linear probability model with survey weights, country-fixed effects, and country-clustered standard errors. Significance levels: * p<.1 ** p<.05 *** p<.01

IMF Lending: Partisanship, Punishment, and Protest 57

partisan allegiance and IMF program participation that is robust across model specifications. In substantive terms, 34.4 percent (95% CI: 31.7–37.2%) of opposition supporters and 30.7 percent (95% CI: 29.2–32.3%) of government supporters conceive the government as biased when the government does not participate in an IMF program – a partisan gap of 3.7 percent (95% CI: 0.5–6.9%). When the government is under an IMF program, this partisan gap increases to 7.4 percent (95% CI: 0.2–14.6%). This is consistent with an intensification of partisan-based distributive politics under IMF SAPs.

Table 5 examines the relationship between partisan allegiance, IMF conditionality, and (the perception of) government bias under various sets of control variables. We find a statistically significant interaction effect between partisan allegiance and IMF conditionality that is robust across model specifications. Because it is difficult to directly read off marginal effects, we predict the outcome for different constellations of the predictors. At the mean of IMF conditionality, the probability that opposition supporters conceive the government as biased is 53.2 percent (95% CI: 49.4–56.9%) and respectively 47.6 percent (95% CI: 43.3–51.9%) for government supporters. This partisan gap widens under a high-conditionality scenario compared to a low-conditionality scenario. These patterns corroborate our argument that partisan allegiance drives distributive politics when governments have lots of opportunities to allocate adjustment burdens of IMF programs. We cannot think of an alternative explanation for these patterns.

In the appendix, we seek to establish the robustness of our findings, considering potential selection at the individual level. Specifically, we include a selection model to predict whether respondents have heard about the IMF. Our excluded instruments – political interest and political knowledge – are strongly significant in the selection model. We find our estimates of interest to be qualitatively unaffected, although less statistically significant in the first two columns (Table A19). Substantively, at the empirical maximum of IMF conditionality, about 74.2 percent (95% CI: 68.6–79.9%) of opposition supporters believe the government is biased, but only 61.8 percent (95% CI: 57.2–66.5%) of government supporters do so.

In addition, we provide another piece of evidence supporting our interpretation. Specifically, we can show that different patterns emerge when people are asked about their impression of the IMF. This outcome is only available for people who have heard about the IMF. We find that partisan differences in the prevalence of bad impressions about the IMF are no less pronounced in countries with IMF exposure compared to countries without IMF exposure (Table A20). A higher number of IMF conditions in an IMF program significantly reduces the partisan gap in negative evaluations of the IMF, compared to a program with fewer conditions (Table A21).

Table 5 Partisan allegiances, IMF conditionality, and government bias in Asian program countries

	(1)		(2)		(3)	
Conditionality	0.081***	(0.007)	0.076***	(0.008)	0.081***	(0.008)
Opposition supporter	−0.305***	(0.113)	−0.331***	(0.112)	−0.315***	(0.112)
(Interaction)	0.034***	(0.010)	0.035***	(0.010)	0.033***	(0.010)
Male			−0.002	(0.020)	0.001	(0.020)
(Logged) age			−0.016	(0.015)	−0.013	(0.015)
Urban			−0.099***	(0.020)	−0.091***	(0.020)
Employed			0.041*	(0.021)	0.039*	(0.021)
Education			−0.031**	(0.015)	−0.030**	(0.015)
Supports democracy			0.033	(0.020)	0.035*	(0.020)
Democracy over growth			−0.017	(0.026)	−0.019	(0.026)
Economy got worse					0.069***	(0.022)
Must obey government					−0.080***	(0.022)
Supports majority rule					−0.009	(0.021)
Observations	2322		2320		2320	
Adjusted R2	0.166		0.180		0.187	

Notes: Dependent variable is government bias. Sample includes only countries with IMF program exposure. Linear probability model with survey weights, country-fixed effects, and country-clustered standard errors. Significance levels: * p<.1 ** p<.05 *** p<.01

IMF Lending: Partisanship, Punishment, and Protest 59

These results suggest that people can identify the government as the main actor responsible for the biased implementation of IMF programs.

4.4 Survey Research on Latin America

We draw on the tenth wave of the Latinobarometer from 2005. We attempt to replicate our findings from the other surveys noting that our measure of partisan allegiance is imperfect because it captures ideological alignment rather than vote choice.

Our outcomes of interest capture perceived deteriorations in the quality of public services. First, the variable PUBLIC EDUCATION WORSENED takes the value of 'one' if the respondent believes that public schools have become worse or much worse over the past year. Second, the variable PUBLIC HEALTH WORSENED mirrors this question concerning the quality of public hospitals. Both items are uniquely valuable for our purpose because they provide a before-after assessment from the same individual, covering a period in which IMF SAP implementation may have plausibly affected these outcomes.

Regarding key predictors, we use the binary indicator OPPOSITION SUPPORTER, constructed by comparing the left-right ideological self-placement of a respondent who voted in the last election to the partisan orientation of the incumbent. In other words, opposition supporters are those voters whose ideological orientation does not overlap with that of the incumbent. This measure is far from perfect. It cannot reliably capture whether respondents voted for an opposition party in the last election. Furthermore, the measure may pick up contemporaneous ideological orientations, rather than ideological orientations at the time of the last election. Respondents may have changed their ideology because of certain government actions during IMF program implementation. However, building on the comparative politics literature, we assume that ideological predispositions do not change rapidly and therefore the measure should pick up long-term partisan allegiances (Lavine, Johnston, and Steenbergen 2012).

As to predictors at the country level, we include the fractional variable IMF EXPOSURE indicating the proportion of years over the past three years in which a country has been under an IMF program. In addition, we count the number of binding conditions, averaged over the three years before the survey year, mirroring the approach taken for the Asian Barometer. We then include interaction terms between the individual-level covariates and the country-level covariates, which allows us to study whether the link between partisan allegiances and public service dissatisfaction is affected by IMF program participation.

In choosing our control variables, we try to match the preceding analyses as much as possible. The barebones model includes country-fixed effects, while subsequent models include demographic characteristics, attitudes, values, and beliefs. Individual demographics include male, age, parental education, years of education, an index of civic engagement (counting the number of memberships in various civil associations), an index of wealth (counting the number of items that a household possesses), and an information index (counting the number of media that a respondent uses). Attitudes, values, and beliefs include support for democracy, support for the market economy, dissatisfaction with presidential performance, and the perception of government corruption. The appendix presents variable definitions and descriptive statistics for all variables (Table A4).

After presenting illustrative evidence and bivariate t-tests, we run linear probability models with country-fixed effects and survey weights. We cluster standard errors by country. As before, testing our argument requires including a cross-level interaction. This again assumes that individual-level mechanisms can be mediated by the country-level difference in IMF program participation and the design of IMF programs.

4.4.1 Illustrative Results

Across our outcomes of interest, we find no significant partisan differences comparing cases under IMF programs and cases without IMF programs. Neither do we find a noticeable change in partisan differences when we compare low-conditionality programs to high-conditionality programs (Figure 22).

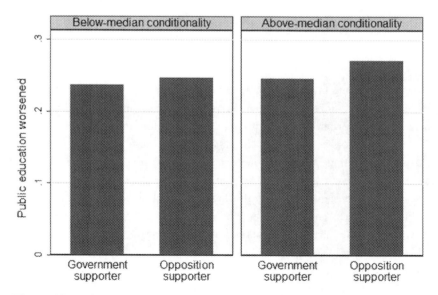

Figure 22 Partisan allegiance, IMF conditionality, and perceived deterioration of public schools

IMF Lending: Partisanship, Punishment, and Protest

Table 6 Partisan allegiances, IMF program exposure, and respondent evaluations of public services in Latin America

	Public education worsened (1)		Health services worsened (2)	
IMF exposure	0.273***	(0.019)	0.105***	(0.013)
Opposition supporter	0.028	(0.026)	0.011	(0.019)
(Interaction)	0.007	(0.032)	−0.007	(0.024)
(Logged) age	0.119***	(0.018)	0.115***	(0.021)
Male	−0.029**	(0.012)	−0.035**	(0.014)
Parental education	0.018***	(0.005)	0.006	(0.005)
Education	0.007	(0.010)	−0.004	(0.008)
Civic engagement index	0.000	(0.008)	0.005	(0.009)
Wealth index	−0.005	(0.003)	−0.003	(0.003)
Information index	0.002	(0.001)	0.001	(0.002)
Supports democracy	−0.034**	(0.014)	−0.032**	(0.013)
Supports market economy	−0.008	(0.011)	−0.025**	(0.009)
Dissatisfied with president	0.105***	(0.012)	0.120***	(0.019)
Officials are corrupt	0.034***	(0.009)	0.057***	(0.007)
Observations	8120		8135	
Adjusted R2	0.072		0.076	

Notes: Dependent variables are shown in the column heads. Linear probability model with survey weights, country-fixed effects, and country-clustered standard errors. Significance levels: * $p<.1$ ** $p<.05$ *** $p<.01$

This could be due to several reasons. It may be that our proxy of partisan allegiance is too rough. It may also be that IMF programs do not drive partisan differences in these outcomes, in part because these outcomes are too remote from IMF policy demands. We now probe these patterns further using multivariate analysis.

4.4.2 Regression Results

Table 6 shows the relationship between partisan allegiances, IMF program exposure, and our two evaluative outcomes of interest. Two findings stand out. First, the extent of perceived deterioration of public services is generally higher where countries have been exposed to IMF programs. This can be seen by inspecting the coefficient estimates for IMF exposure and those for the interaction term. Second, opposition supporters tend to be no more dissatisfied with public services than government supporters. This result holds both in the absence of IMF program exposure, as well as in the presence of program

62 *International Relations*

exposure. Before we draw definitive conclusions about this issue, we turn to our subsample analysis of countries with IMF program exposure.

Table 7 shows the relationship between partisan allegiances, average IMF conditionality, and the two evaluative outcomes in Latin American program countries. We find that opposition supporters tend to be marginally more likely to have worse evaluations of public services in these IMF program countries. This partisan difference appears to be unaffected by the stringency of IMF conditionality. In sum, this set of results provides the weakest support for our argument among all our analyses. We will revisit how to interpret these results in the conclusion, given our other findings.

4.5 World Values Survey

We draw on the combined longitudinal dataset covering six waves of the World Values Survey (WVS). The WVS dataset contains survey responses of 422,150 individuals from 102 countries in the period from 1981 to 2019

Table 7 Partisan allegiances, IMF conditionality, and respondent evaluations of public services in Latin America

	Public education worsened (1)		Health services worsened (2)	
Average conditionality	−0.031***	(0.001)	−0.012***	(0.001)
Opposition supporter	0.029	(0.020)	0.033*	(0.016)
(Interaction)	0.000	(0.001)	−0.001	(0.001)
(Logged) age	0.120***	(0.023)	0.101***	(0.026)
Male	−0.025*	(0.013)	−0.038**	(0.014)
Parental education	0.020**	(0.007)	0.006	(0.005)
Education	0.012	(0.012)	−0.007	(0.010)
Civic engagement index	0.006	(0.009)	0.006	(0.009)
Wealth index	−0.004	(0.004)	−0.003	(0.003)
Information index	0.002	(0.001)	0.000	(0.002)
Supports democracy	−0.035**	(0.013)	−0.035**	(0.011)
Supports market economy	−0.014	(0.016)	−0.018*	(0.009)
Dissatisfied with president	0.098***	(0.015)	0.101***	(0.021)
Officials are corrupt	0.031***	(0.008)	0.051***	(0.008)
Observations	6694		6704	
Adjusted R2	0.068		0.077	

Notes: Dependent variables are shown in the column heads. Linear probability model with survey weights, country-fixed effects, and country-clustered standard errors. Significance levels: * p<.1 ** p<.05 *** p<.01

(Inglehart et al. 2014). The dataset is repeated cross-sections, as individuals are not tracked systematically over successive waves. Not all countries participate in all waves and hence feature in the dataset only in select years. We do not conduct all analyses on the WVS dataset because it lacks a clear measure of partisan allegiance and does not include questions about experience with IMF SAPs that could directly address our research questions. However, one advantage of using the WVS data is to allow us to probe the generalizability of our patterns across all world regions while using the same measures of partisan allegiance, self-reported hardships, and protest.

An even more important benefit of the WVS dataset is its broad coverage, which affords us the possibility to test an important macro-level confounder. Specifically, when comparing outcomes across partisans in countries under an IMF program and countries not under any IMF program, we cannot be sure that our results indeed capture the impacts of IMF programs and not the impacts of the financial crises that typically precede these programs. This selection problem is well-known to macro-level researchers of IMF effectiveness (Forster et al. 2019; Lang 2021; Stubbs et al. 2020a). In our context, it still affects how we interpret the widening partisan gap in relevant outcomes: Are they specific to country participation in an IMF program? Or do they occur also when countries undergo economically challenging times that would force governments to implement similar adjustment policies? Even though our focus is on comparing distributive outcomes and political behaviors between government supporters and opposition supporters, we believe it is important to understand how we should interpret the evidence of intensified partisan politics under the circumstances of IMF program participation.

Given the larger country sample of the WVS dataset, we can explicitly account for financial crises as the main confounder for government participation in IMF programs. We are agnostic as to whether financial crises on their own intensify partisan politics, although it is quite likely that they do. Our key argument is that where countries try to resolve such crises with the IMF, partisan politics will be significantly more intense, given the additional adjustment burdens of IMF programs that governments will seek to impose on opposition supporters. In summary, we compare partisan gaps in relevant outcomes across different macro-level contexts (Table 8). First, the no-crisis-no-program scenario is the most benign, reflecting the lowest-possible level of partisan politics. Second, if a crisis hits, partisan politics may increase, particularly where governments face adjustment costs that can be targeted to specific partisan groups. Third, if a crisis hits and the government agrees to an IMF program, partisan politics increases significantly, given that governments

64 *International Relations*

Table 8 Macro-level contexts in the global longitudinal dataset

	No IMF program	**IMF program**
No financial crisis	No-crisis-no-program scenario: business as usual	Incumbent-driven program
Financial crisis	Self-help scenario	IMF-supported adjustment program

face specific demands like trimming expenditure, cutting public-sector jobs, and privatizing state companies that can be implemented in a partisan-biased fashion.[7]

We now introduce the key variables for the WVS analysis. We identify two individual-level outcomes with good time-series cross-section coverage that capture the extent of experienced hardship of respondents. First, we use the DEPRIVATION INDEX to capture the extent to which the respondent (and their family) have respectively gone without enough food to eat, medicine or treatment, and cash income in the past twelve months. The index ranges from zero (never any deprivation in any dimension) to nine (often deprived for all three essential items). Second, we measure the INCOME GROUP of a respondent, using an ordinal variable from the WVS survey with three income brackets corresponding to low income, middle income, and high income.[8]

Turning to macro-level predictors, we measure the extent to which countries suffer from financial crises. In our preferred specification, we measure the exposure of a country to financial crisis in the three-year period before the survey year (Laeven and Valencia 2013). In robustness checks, we use a dummy variable that indicates whether the country suffered a financial crisis two years before the survey year. IMF program exposure is the second macro-level variable. We identify countries that were under an IMF program in any of the three years before the survey year. In robustness checks, we use a dummy capturing IMF program participation lagged by two years relative to the survey year. We draw the data for IMF program participation from the IMF Monitor Database (Kentikelenis, Stubbs, and King 2016).

Turning to the micro level, we follow an approach similar to the Latinobarometer in which we constructed a measure of partisan allegiance by combining the ideological self-placement of the individual with data about the partisan ideology of the incumbent government. We distinguish between left-wing partisans and

---

[7] The fourth scenario is an "incumbent driven program" which we disregard as we intend to control for the incidence of a financial crisis.

[8] Other research has also taken this approach (Reinsberg et al. 2023).

IMF Lending: Partisanship, Punishment, and Protest 65

right-wing partisans. We consider individuals as left-wing partisans if they place themselves on the lower half of the ten-item scale and as right-wing partisans if they place themselves on the upper half of the ten-item scale (*E033*). For government ideology, we draw on the Database of Political Institutions to distinguish left-wing governments, centrist governments, and right-wing governments and measure the share of years under left-wing governments in the three years before the survey (Scartascini, Cruz, and Keefer 2018). To construct a measure of partisan misalignment, we calculate the squared difference between being a left-wing individual and having a left-wing government for at least two years out of three years.[9] The measure takes the value of one for OPPOSITION SUPPORTERS and the value of zero for government supporters. To be sure, the measure cannot tell us if people actively supported the party with which they align but captures the potential for people to do so given their ideological alignment.

Because we include country-wave fixed effects, we account for the generic effect of any macro-level confounder that might affect our outcomes of interest uniformly for all partisans. Therefore, we only need to control for micro-level confounders. We include a range of micro-level variables to match as closely as possible our regional barometer analyses while avoiding variables with many missing values. Balancing these criteria, our first set of demographic variables includes (logged) age, male, married, educated (at least medium level), political interest, under-employment (being unemployed or being employed less than full-time), and the number of people in the household. The second set of controls captures values, beliefs, and preferences: demand for democracy, priority for growth, preference for equality, and confidence in government. To ease interpretation, we dichotomize variables at the mid-point of the scale where they are not already binary. The supplemental appendix presents variable definitions and descriptive statistics for all the variables (Table A5).

4.5.1 Illustrative Evidence

Figure 23 shows the extent of deprivation after a financial crisis as experienced by respondents with different partisan allegiances. The left panel includes countries that attempted crisis resolution without IMF programs, while the right panel includes countries with IMF programs. The results are striking. Even under highly turbulent times of financial crisis, there is no apparent partisan difference in deprivation in countries without IMF involvement.

---

[9] Formally, the measure is computed as $O=(L-l)^2$, where O stands for opposition supporter, L for whether the individual is left, and l for whether the country had a left-wing government for most of the pre-survey period. For example, a right-wing individual ($L=0$) under left-wing government ($l=1$) will be coded as an opposition supporter ($O=(-1)^2=1$), while a left-wing individual ($L=1$) would not ($O=0$).

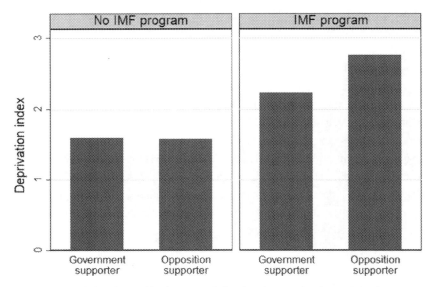

Figure 23 Partisan allegiance and deprivation under financial crises.

In contrast, there is a significant partisan difference in deprivation in crisis-affected countries that involved the IMF. While government supporters also appear to suffer from increased hardship under IMF programs, the burdens for opposition supporters are inordinately higher. The partisan difference in deprivation is 0.528 (95% CI: 0.336–0.722) – a tangible difference given the ten-point range of the index points that is also statistically significant in a t-test ($p<0.001$). These patterns suggest that governments under IMF-mandated programs lump additional adjustment burdens onto opposition supporters. The patterns also suggest that the intensification of partisan politics is not the inevitable consequence of financial turmoil but requires IMF-mandated policies that facilitate such partisan politics.

While we focus on deprivation as our main outcome of interest, the patterns look similar for income as an alternative outcome (Figure A11). As confirmed by t-tests, opposition supporters have lower income than government supporters if their country faced a financial crisis *and* the country underwent an IMF program but not if the crisis-affected country avoided the IMF program.

4.5.2 Regression Analysis

Table 9 shows the relationship between partisan allegiances and deprivation in the context of financial crises, distinguishing cases of IMF programs and cases without IMF programs. In line with the illustrative evidence, we find a significantly

	Crisis resolution with IMF program						Crisis resolution without program					
	(1)		(2)		(3)		(4)		(5)		(6)	
Financial crisis	–	–	–	–	–	–	−0.947**	(0.375)	−1.025***	(0.356)	−0.910**	(0.368)
Opposition supporter	−0.029	(0.057)	0.025	(0.054)	0.011	(0.048)	0.049	(0.035)	0.038	(0.035)	0.018	(0.035)
(Interaction)	0.400***	(0.111)	0.238**	(0.096)	0.266***	(0.081)	−0.113	(0.255)	−0.126	(0.241)	−0.115	(0.243)
Male			−0.096**	(0.037)	−0.104**	(0.041)			0.040	(0.030)	0.033	(0.031)
(Logged) age			0.009	(0.113)	0.001	(0.113)			−0.325***	(0.113)	−0.321***	(0.114)
Married			−0.254***	(0.047)	−0.246***	(0.050)			−0.261***	(0.046)	−0.249***	(0.050)
Household size			0.104***	(0.021)	0.103***	(0.023)			0.107***	(0.019)	0.108***	(0.020)
Underemployed			0.296***	(0.062)	0.293***	(0.060)			0.245***	(0.037)	0.250***	(0.042)
Educated			−0.548***	(0.082)	−0.513***	(0.087)			−0.565***	(0.076)	−0.548***	(0.083)
Politically interested			0.065	(0.039)	0.095**	(0.041)			0.047	(0.053)	0.065	(0.052)
Demand for democracy					−0.198**	(0.077)					−0.271***	(0.081)
Priority for growth					0.110**	(0.045)					0.049	(0.030)
Preference for equality					0.169**	(0.065)					0.141***	(0.048)
Confidence in government					−0.124	(0.073)					−0.075	(0.064)
Observations	40305		39480		34637		90557		86193		73669	
Countries	24		24		23		42		42		40	
Adjusted R2	0.175		0.197		0.209		0.181		0.205		0.215	

Notes: Dependent variable is the deprivation index. Financial crisis is measured as the share of years with a financial crisis over the three years before the survey. Linear probability model with survey weights, country-fixed effects, year-fixed effects, and country-clustered standard errors in parentheses. Significance levels: * p<.1 ** p<.05 *** p<.01.

68   *International Relations*

positive interaction effect between the incidence of financial crisis and being an
opposition supporter, but only in the subsample of countries with IMF program
participation. Where countries facing financial turmoil attempted to resolve their
crises without IMF programs, we do not find a significant partisan gap concerning
experienced deprivation.

Model predictions underscore the substantive significance of these differences. Focusing on countries that experienced financial turmoil in the three
years before the survey, the partisan gap in deprivation is estimated to be at least
0.266 (95% CI: 0.104–0.428) on a ten-point scale. In crisis countries without
IMF involvement, this partisan gap is indistinguishable from zero. Our findings
are based on up to forty-two countries and nine survey years, which eases
concerns that they could be driven by outlying cases. Moreover, the results
are robust to different sets of individual-level control variables. The estimates of
the control variables are consistent with expectations that deprivation is more
prevalent among women (especially during IMF programs), larger households,
un(der)employed people, and less educated people.

In the appendix, we demonstrate the robustness of these findings to alternative
measures and modeling choices. First, we show similar results when using the
income group as the outcome variable (Table A22). We find that crisis resolution
with an IMF program is associated with significantly lower income among opposition supporters relative to opposition supporters. However, the partisan gap in
incomes does not exist for crisis countries that did not turn to the IMF. The results
are based on a high number of countries across several survey waves. Second, we
probe whether results hold for a narrower timing of macro-events. Specifically, we
capture whether a country underwent a financial crisis two years before the survey,
which is the year before respondents are asked to assess whether they suffered any
hardships. We use the same operationalization to capture whether a country had an
IMF program. We continue to find a strongly bifurcated pattern whereby the
partisan gap in experienced deprivation is large for crisis countries that participated
in an IMF program but indistinguishable from zero when the country did not
undergo an IMF program (Table A23). For the results on income, the findings are
less clear-cut, although they tend to reproduce a larger partisan gap in the crisis
scenario with IMF participation (Table A24).

5 How Distributive Politics under IMF Programs Affect Protest

We now examine how distributional politics in the context of IMF SAPs affects
protest. We briefly recap that our core theoretical argument highlights the role of
IMF adjustment lending amplifying pre-existing distributional inequalities in
many societies. As part of these agreements, governments will need to make

IMF Lending: Partisanship, Punishment, and Protest   69

unpopular cuts and agonizing economic reforms. Yet, they retain discretion in how to meet many of these targets. We argue that they will seek to maintain their winning coalition and primarily lump adjustment burdens onto opposition supporters. We expect that this amplification of distributional politics under IMF adjustment lending will lead opposition supporters to protest more. We begin with an illustrative case study of Kenya. We then provide econometric tests of our arguments first presenting results from Afrobarometer, Asian Barometer, and Latinobarometer, followed by a probe of generalizability using the WVS.

5.1 Kenya as an Illustrative Case

We illuminate our argument with evidence from a within-case study of Kenya. With few exceptions (Azam 2008), existing research indicates that many Kenyan politicians utilize distributional politics, often organized along ethnic lines, to favor their supporters across a wide range of policy areas including spending on health, education, and road construction (Beiser-McGrath, Müller-Crepon, and Pengl 2020; Burgess et al. 2015; Harris and Posner 2019; Makoloo 2005).

We conduct a most-similar intertemporal case comparison. Kenya is a valuable case for our analysis because while the country was under IMF assistance, partisan control of the government changed. Despite facing similar external demands, both governments implemented IMF-mandated reforms differently because of their different partisan support bases. Both undertook a variety of distributional approaches to protect their supporters from IMF adjustment burdens.

To highlight how IMF SAPs provide political leaders with increased opportunities to alter distributional outcomes in line with political allegiances, we discuss how the two consecutive administrations implemented IMF-mandated civil-service retrenchment measures. We generate our insights from an original review of local news media and secondary literature on Kenyan politics under structural adjustment. While our discussion focuses on civil-service retrenchment, as an example of an area where IMF reforms inflict burdens upon society, there is also evidence about the politically biased allocation of benefits of IMF-sponsored reforms such as parastatal appointments, the privatization of SOEs, the building of infrastructure projects, and the awarding of contracts (Kisero 2003; The East African Standard 2007; The Nation 2009).

5.1.1 Moi Administration (1997–2002)

Daniel arap Moi, leader of the Kenya African National Union (KANU), took office after the death of Jomo Kenyatta in 1978. Moi had a relatively narrow support base, relying on the Kalenjin ethnic group and minority groups from the Rift Valley.

70 *International Relations*

Moi's Kalenjin group benefited from plum jobs in the civil service, army, and SOEs (Wrong 2010, 51).

Moi agreed to two Extended Credit Facility loans with the IMF – respectively for 1996–1999 and 2000–2003, \$216 million each. A key IMF demand was to retrench a total of 32,348 public-sector workers by 2002, with 25,783 civil servants slated for dismissal by October 2000 (Kamau 2000). Other areas of the package included parastatal reform, price liberalization, and divestiture of public enterprises (IMF 1996).

Moi had ultimate responsibility for the retrenchment of civil servants – a task that he delegated to his permanent secretaries (Warigi 2000). These appointees discriminated in the hiring of civil servants (The Nation 2014); there is no reason to believe they would behave any differently in their dismissal of employees. Under the threat of a national strike and facing the upcoming re-election in 1997, his government acceded to the demands of about 260,000 teachers for a 150–200 percent pay rise in October 1997 (The Nation 2013). To further this sense of unfairness, Moi excluded the security services and teachers from the IMF-mandated retrenchment in 2000.

The contradictory set of criteria for targeting staff to retrench included age, gender, health, the record of past service, and academic and professional qualifications (Otieno 2009, 66). In practice, these criteria particularly favored Kikuyu and Kalenjin ethnic groups, who tended to be more educated and have better health outcomes compared to minority ethnic groups, and men who were better educated than women (Otieno 2009, 66). At the same time, the government sought to increase the salaries of civil servants who remained in government employment, effectively concentrating the benefits of employment even during the midst of adjustment lending (Daily Nation 2000).

Kenyans challenged the politically driven implementation of retrenchment. Societal groups like the Retrenchees Welfare Association claimed that the process was "biased, unfair, political and riddled with irregularities." They objected to "the rush to beat the deadline and the use of poorly selected committees dominated by members who gave room to prejudice, witch-hunting and ethnicity ... and claimed that certain political affiliations and communities were being favored in the exercise" (Sunday Nation 2000). These critiques chime with reporting elsewhere about the promotion of under-qualified individuals who are co-ethnics of senior managers (Wrong 2010). Even junior ministers in the governing party, like assistant minister Charfano Guyo Mokku, said that "the civil-service retrenchment program was discriminatory, flawed and unfair to certain ethnic communities" (Sunday Nation 2000).

IMF Lending: Partisanship, Punishment, and Protest   71

National Labour Party chairman Kennedy Kiliku said the retrenchment process was illegal, arguing that "opposition sympathizers were being victimized through retrenchment . . . and that the so-called downsizing was actually 'downsizing' the opposition sympathizers" (Kithi 2000).

Kenyans mobilized to protest civil-service cuts and fiscal austerity (Ellis-Jones 2002, 18). In May 2001, state-employed air traffic controllers in Mombasa airport went on strike demanding better terms of employment and salary increases. In September 2001, Mombasa council workers dumped piles of rubbish on the street all over the city and inside city hall to protest the non-payment of three months salaries (Ellis-Jones 2002, 18). The strike, which lasted for over a week, ended up in running battles with the police. Mombasa was an opposition stronghold. Moi's KANU party received only about a third of the votes across each parliamentary constituency, holding only one of the four Mombasa districts in the 1997 election (Rakodi, Gatabaki-Kamau, and Devas 2000, 160). Moi's administration also withheld the salaries of local government workers in Kakamega, which led to a series of strikes in 2001. Kakamega is in Kenya's Lurambi constituency and was won by opposition politician Newton Kulundu in 1997.

5.1.2 Kibaki Administration (2003–2007)

In late 2002, Moi's nominee Uhuru Kenyatta lost KANU's bid to retain power to opposition leader Mwai Kibaki's National Rainbow Coalition (NARC). While NARC primarily reflected Kibaki's own Kikuyu ethnic group it also included a dozen other ethno-regional parties and represented a broader electoral coalition than the previous Moi administration (Barkan 2004). Kibaki's approach to distributional politics in the context of IMF lending manifested itself in broad-based sectoral and infrastructural initiatives rewarding areas and regions of support with government spending facilitated by the IMF. Kibaki dismissed the heads of parastatal, permanent secretaries, and other high-ranking members of the civil service and those on the judicial bench who had been installed by ex-president Moi.

Kibaki concluded a three-year Extended Credit Facility of over $252 million with the IMF, in exchange for IMF demands to combat corruption in the judiciary, passage of a strengthened anti-corruption bill, reform of parastatals, and civil-service retrenchment (Opiyo 2003a). Notably, Kibaki's administration was tasked with dismissing another 24,000 workers during the period of its loan (Githahu and Omanga 2003).

In his early statements as president, Kibaki demonstrated his commitment to representing all forty-two ethnic communities in his new government

(Ochieng 2002). He resisted calls by the IMF to cut civil-service spending during his first year in office (Opiyo 2003b). In his first ten months, his administration already spent more on wages than the allotted amount for the year in the IMF Medium Term Expenditure Framework (Opiyo 2003a). The Kibaki administration also sought to enlarge portions of the civil service as part of its approach to distributional politics (The Nation 2009). It continued with the commitment of the previous Moi administration promising increases in teacher salaries, although the IMF warned that this would undermine progress toward the envisaged cuts in the public-sector wage bill (Kamau 2003).

While Kibaki's administration was more reluctant to engage in targeted cuts given his broad coalition of support, protests did take place. For example, on March 3, 2005, a group of civil society organizations used the occurrence of a mini-ministerial World Trade Organization conference taking place at a luxury Kenyan South Coast resort to demand greater African participation at the conference in general and protest the role of international financial institutions in Kenya in particular. About 500 protesters took part in a peaceful protest, 40 of whom were arrested by the police (CIS 2005).

Kibaki's administration was very sensitive to demands from international institutions which had clear distributional impacts on his support base that could encourage protest, despite potentially benefiting the country overall. For example, the World Bank pressured the Kibaki administration to liberalize the maize market in Kenya to solve its long-standing issues of maize shortages. While unrestricted imports of maize may have helped to solve issues of food security within the country, the government was reluctant to enact these changes because maize farmers in the North Rift would be hardest hit (Opiyo 2003a). Kibaki more than doubled his vote share in the Rift Valley from 20.9 percent to 43 percent in the December 2002 election (Throup 2003). Maintaining the benefits of the status quo to his supporters was one issue that would be at stake in liberalizing the market.

In summary, we find evidence for distributional politics in the context of structural adjustment. Despite facing similar IMF pressures, Moi's narrower coalition base meant that he could target more opposition supporters for cuts in comparison to Kibaki's administration, whose broad coalition made him more reluctant to also make cuts. Facing similar IMF demands, both incumbents used their discretion and implemented IMF-sponsored reforms to protect their partisan supporters, leading to grievances and protests mobilized by opposition supporters.

5.2 Survey Research on Sub-Saharan Africa

We draw on the same sample of respondents from the first wave of the Afrobarometer as in our analysis of pocketbook evaluations. Our binary dependent variable of interest is PROTEST. As detailed in the appendix (Table A2), this is based on a survey question of whether the respondent engaged in protest as a form of political behavior in the past five years. In robustness checks, we construe a broader measure of protest by including protest inclinations. This broader measure then includes whether respondents protested or considered engaging in protest. The choice of operationalization does not alter our findings.

To examine whether partisan-biased implementation of IMF SAPs drives protest, two strategies are available. The first is to examine whether individuals who feel they are worse off due to the IMF SAP are more likely to protest. This offers a straightforward test of our argument but may be problematic to the extent that evaluations may be tainted by political allegiances because of perceptive biases rather than objective discrimination. The second strategy mirrors our analysis of pocketbook evaluations. Here we include predictors at two levels of analysis and their multiplicative interaction. At the individual level, we capture the partisan alignment of the respondent with the incumbent government. We use the dichotomous variable OPPOSITION SUPPORTER, which indicates whether a respondent supported an opposition party rather than the government party in the past election. We drop individuals that did not support any party. At the country level, we draw on two measures. The first is a binary indicator for whether a country had been under an IMF SAP in any of the four years before the survey date, which allows us to compare partisan-induced protest in IMF program countries and non-program countries.[10] The second is a count of the total number of conditions in survey countries with IMF programs. As the number of conditions is a proxy for the total adjustment burden, governments will have greater scope for inflicting pain on their opponents in programs with many conditions, which are therefore called 'high-discretion programs'.

We use three sets of control variables based on considerations for parsimony, and comparability across barometer surveys with an emphasis on plausible confounders. The first is a stripped-down model without individual-level controls but only country-fixed effects. Therefore, our analysis only models variation across respondents within survey countries. The second set of controls

---

[10] This operational choice considers that governments sometimes must fulfill IMF conditions before being able to access any funds. Once governments attempt to implement these "prior actions," there is a theoretical possibility of protest that would be captured by the five-year backward-looking survey item.

74   *International Relations*

adds standard demographic characteristics that are known to affect protest (Gurr 1969; Robertson and Teitelbaum 2011; Tilly 1978). These variables include the (logged) age of the respondent, and dummies for whether the respondent is male, employed, educated, and lives in an urban area. We also measure unconditional support for democracy. In the third set, we include indicators for whether the respondent believes the government performs poorly; whether respondents think the economy is doing worse than twelve months ago; whether respondents prefer to not retrench the public sector even if this was costly to the country; whether the respondent believes the government is run to benefit the few; whether the respondent perceives the right to free assembly has become more restrictive; and whether the respondent believes society has become more unequal compared to the previous regime.[11]

Given the potential for unobserved country heterogeneity, we estimate linear probability models with country-fixed effects. These also have the advantage of ease of interpretation, compared to non-linear models. While multi-level random-effect models would be a principal alternative, their assumptions of normally distributed random intercepts for countries are unlikely to hold in our small samples. We note here that our results are qualitatively unaffected by this modeling choice.

Another choice refers to the sample of respondents. While people in principle could protest because of the IMF SAP even without knowing about the program, we prefer to continue using the sample of individuals who have heard about the IMF SAP to maximize consistency with our analysis of IMF SAP evaluations. More importantly, we can only link dissatisfaction with the IMF SAP to protest behavior for individuals who have heard about the IMF SAP and provided an evaluation of its pocketbook effects.

5.2.1 Illustrative Evidence

We proceed with simple comparisons and bivariate t-tests. Figure 24 shows the average prevalence of protest in sub-Saharan program countries depending on whether or not respondents consider that the IMF SAP has made their life worse. We find a remarkable difference in protest behavior across both groups. While 18.6 percent (95% CI: 17.2–20.0%) of those who think that the IMF SAP made their life worse protest, it is only 15.4 percent (95% CI: 14.0–16.8%) of those who think otherwise. The percentage-point difference of 3.2 percent is statistically significant according to a t-test ($p<0.01$).

---

[11] Since perceptions that government is run by the few could also be a result of being adversely affected by IMF SAPs, this variable could introduce post-treatment bias. We verify that results without this variable are virtually identical.

IMF Lending: Partisanship, Punishment, and Protest 75

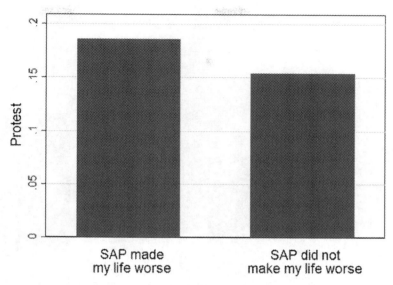

Figure 24 Pocketbook evaluations of IMF SAPs and protest

Of course, it may again be the case that, for reasons that we cannot capture, respondents may both hold negative views about the IMF SAP and be more likely to protest. This would make the relationship of interest spurious. Our main remedy to this challenge is to exploit variations in the number of conditions in IMF SAPs. Specifically, programs with more conditions imply a higher burden of adjustment that governments can lump onto opposition supporters. The increased opportunity for partisan politics in this case should affect partisan differences in outcomes. Figure 25 confirms our expectation. We find a larger difference in protest frequencies depending on how people evaluate the pocketbook effect of the IMF SAP in the high-conditionality scenario, compared to the same difference in the low-conditionality scenario. In the former, the difference is 12.1 percent ($p<0.0001$), but only 2.9 percent in the latter ($p=0.51$).[12]

An alternative approach is to relate protest to partisanship and exploit variation in IMF exposure and program design. Figure 26 shows the results. We find that among countries not under an IMF program, the frequency of protest is roughly the same across different partisan groups – with only a difference of 1.7 percent ($p=0.60$). In contrast, in countries with an IMF SAP, opposition supporters have a significantly higher likelihood of protest than government supporters. A t-test confirms that the percentage-point

---

[12] Here and in subsequent occurrences, these percentages should be read as absolute differences in percentage points.

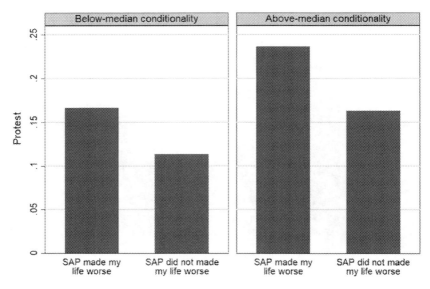

Figure 25 Program design, pocketbook evaluations of IMF SAPs, and protest

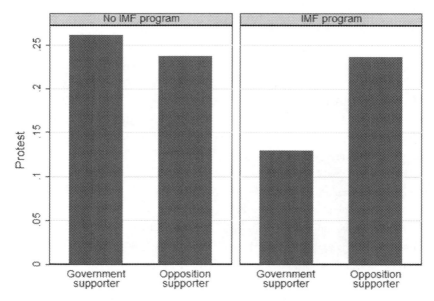

Figure 26 Partisan allegiances, IMF program exposure, and protest

difference of 10.7 percent is significant (p<0.001). These patterns provide strong suggestive evidence for the protest-inducing effect of distributive politics facilitated by government exposure to IMF programs.

IMF Lending: Partisanship, Punishment, and Protest

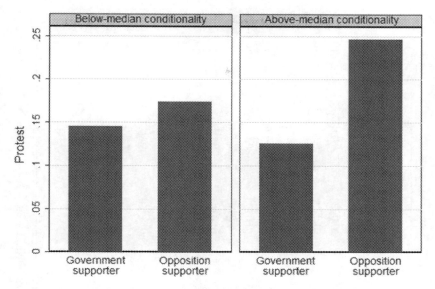

Figure 27 Partisan allegiances, IMF conditionality, and protest

Figure 27 shows the relationship between partisan allegiances, IMF conditionality, and protest. Exploiting program design assumes that the scope for distributive politics increases as governments face more extensive burdens of adjustment. Our illustrative evidence using countries under IMF programs is consistent with this expectation. We find that the partisan-induced gap in average protest is higher in the high-conditionality scenario, compared to a low-conditionality scenario. In the former case, the percentage-point difference in protest across partisan groups is 12.1 percent ($p<0.001$), while it is only 2.9 percent ($p=0.51$) and statistically insignificant in the latter case. Furthermore, protest frequencies are relatively higher in the high-conditionality cases.

5.2.2 Regression Analysis

We now scrutinize the above relationships using multivariate analysis. Table 10 shows that people who feel adversely affected by IMF SAPs are more likely to protest: their likelihood of protest is 14.9 percent (95% CI: 7.5–22.3%), compared to 11.4 percent (95% CI: 3.4–19.4%) for those who do not think that the IMF SAP made their life worse. These results hold across different model specifications ($p<0.01$).

In the next step, we identify differential treatment by the government based on partisan allegiances during the implementation of IMF SAPs as a source of grievance-induced protest. Since the question on protest is not formulated concerning IMF SAPs, we exploit variation in exposure to IMF programs.

Table 10 Negative pocketbook evaluation of IMF SAPs and protest in African program countries

	(1)		(2)		(3)	
SAP made my life worse	0.061***	(0.007)	0.038***	(0.008)	0.039***	(0.008)
Male			0.038**	(0.011)	0.038**	(0.011)
(Logged) age			−0.079**	(0.028)	−0.078**	(0.028)
Urban			0.025	(0.015)	0.026	(0.015)
Unemployed			0.049**	(0.017)	0.049**	(0.016)
Educated			−0.022**	(0.008)	−0.022**	(0.008)
Radio listener			−0.007*	(0.003)	−0.007*	(0.003)
Politically interested			0.068***	(0.012)	0.067***	(0.012)
Politically knowledgeable			0.048**	(0.014)	0.048**	(0.014)
Satisfied with democracy			0.017	(0.014)	0.014	(0.011)
Supports free market			0.014**	(0.006)	0.014*	(0.006)
Supports capitalism			0.007	(0.005)	0.007	(0.005)
Supports public sector			0.004	(0.010)	0.004	(0.009)
Supports privatization			0.013	(0.016)	0.013	(0.015)
Worse now than 12 months ago					−0.007*	(0.003)
Worse in 12 months					−0.012	(0.009)
Dissatisfied with president					−0.025	(0.037)
Observations	14092		13850		13850	
Adjusted R2	0.091		0.118		0.118	

Notes: Dependent variable is protest. Linear probability models with survey weights, country-fixed effects, and country-clustered standard errors. Significance levels: * p<.1 ** p<.05 *** p<.01

IMF Lending: Partisanship, Punishment, and Protest 79

Table 11 shows the results from split-sample regressions by program exposure. We find that partisan allegiance tends to be positively related to protest when the country had IMF exposure, although the coefficient is statistically significant only in one model. In contrast, we do not find any effect of being an opposition supporter on protest when the country had not been under an IMF SAP. In other words, the differences across partisan groups concerning the propensity for protest are larger for program countries than for countries not under an IMF program. Despite lacking statistical significance, the findings are consistent with our argument that IMF program participation can increase the prevalence of protest due to intensified distributive politics.

A final step is to examine partisan-induced differences in protest exploiting variation in IMF conditionality. Our relevant sample is all countries with an IMF SAP. Table 12 shows the results from split-sample regressions at the median of IMF conditionality for program countries. We find that partisan allegiance is significantly related to protest when the government has faced an above-median number of IMF conditions, but not for a below-median number of IMF conditions, which is exactly what the distributive politics argument would lead us to expect. Substantively, the difference across partisan groups is 4.9 percentage points ($p<0.01$) in the former scenario. In the latter scenario, it is larger but not precisely estimated.

5.2.3 Threats to Inference, Robustness Tests, and Further Analyses

We now probe the robustness of our findings and address potential threats to inference. One issue – that perceptive biases rather than objective hardships affect IMF SAP evaluations – is less problematic in the study of protest. This is because even perceptions can have real consequences concerning protest. However, it would be interesting to know whether partisan-related protest in the context of IMF SAPs is primarily due to unfair treatment or the perception thereof. Therefore, we examine how deprivation – under different scenarios of IMF conditionality – affects protest. In the appendix, we confirm that as conditionality increases, more deprivation increases the likelihood of protest (Table A25).[13]

As our analyses so far only included respondents who are aware of the IMF SAP, findings could be liable to selection bias. This would be the case if unobserved respondent characteristics were to drive both their awareness of the IMF SAP and their decision to protest. We therefore model IMF SAP

---

[13] We also augment the model using partisanship and its interaction with IMF conditionality. As the partisan-related terms are insignificant in this augmented model, we infer that protest is indeed driven by objective hardships, which themselves are driven by partisan allegiances.

Table 11 Partisan allegiances, IMF program, and protest in African program countries

	IMF program						No IMF program					
	(1)		(2)		(3)		(4)		(5)		(6)	
Opposition supporter	0.119*	(0.054)	0.100	(0.052)	0.090	(0.051)	0.024	(0.075)	0.018	(0.083)	0.026	(0.068)
Male			−0.008	(0.044)	−0.007	(0.044)			0.046**	(0.003)	0.048	(0.008)
(Logged) age			−0.041	(0.039)	−0.037	(0.038)			−0.225	(0.041)	−0.232	(0.050)
Urban			0.104***	(0.013)	0.105***	(0.013)			0.071*	(0.008)	0.066	(0.011)
Unemployed			0.040	(0.047)	0.041	(0.047)			0.011	(0.008)	0.006	(0.012)
Educated			−0.014	(0.023)	−0.017	(0.022)			−0.063	(0.019)	−0.063	(0.017)
Radio listener			0.029	(0.017)	0.029	(0.017)			−0.038	(0.019)	−0.036	(0.022)
Politically interested			0.051**	(0.015)	0.051**	(0.014)			0.040	(0.051)	0.036	(0.043)
Politically knowledgeable			0.042	(0.022)	0.039	(0.023)			0.050	(0.024)	0.053	(0.023)
Satisfied with democracy			−0.008	(0.029)	−0.004	(0.030)			0.037	(0.026)	0.032	(0.017)
Supports free market			0.021	(0.028)	0.020	(0.026)			−0.007	(0.010)	−0.003	(0.014)
Supports capitalism			0.004	(0.020)	0.003	(0.020)			−0.034	(0.028)	−0.032	(0.024)
Supports public sector			0.023	(0.019)	0.025	(0.019)			0.023	(0.029)	0.016	(0.035)
Supports privatization			0.004	(0.009)	0.005	(0.008)			0.009	(0.025)	0.010	(0.023)
Worse now than 12 months ago					−0.031	(0.016)					0.055	(0.041)
Worse in 12 months					−0.016	(0.018)					−0.035	(0.026)
Dissatisfied with president					0.051**	(0.015)					−0.273*	(0.023)
Observations	2323		2300		2300		673		673		673	
Adjusted R2	0.049		0.076		0.078		0.11		0.152		0.159	

Notes: Dependent variable is protest. Sample includes only individuals who are aware of the IMF SAP. Linear probability models with survey weights, country-fixed effects, and country-clustered standard errors. Significance levels: * p<.1 ** p<.05 *** p<.01

Table 12 Partisan allegiances, IMF program, and protest in African program countries

	Above-median conditionality			Below-median conditionality		
	(1)	(2)	(3)	(4)	(5)	(6)
Opposition supporter	0.084**	0.051*	0.049***	0.146	0.133	0.123
	(0.003)	(0.006)	(0.000)	(0.100)	(0.099)	(0.100)
Male		0.016	0.017		−0.024	−0.023
		(0.023)	(0.022)		(0.069)	(0.069)
(Logged) age		−0.080	−0.077		−0.005	−0.003
		(0.041)	(0.041)		(0.050)	(0.048)
Urban		0.117**	0.115**		0.096**	0.099**
		(0.007)	(0.003)		(0.021)	(0.023)
Unemployed		0.005	0.009		0.146	0.149
		(0.013)	(0.017)		(0.066)	(0.066)
Educated		−0.034	−0.033		−0.003	−0.006
		(0.061)	(0.061)		(0.022)	(0.024)
Radio listener		0.008	0.007		0.050**	0.049**
		(0.015)	(0.014)		(0.014)	(0.013)
Politically interested		0.041*	0.041*		0.055*	0.055*
		(0.005)	(0.004)		(0.021)	(0.020)
Politically knowledgeable		0.080	0.080		0.019	0.016
		(0.020)	(0.020)		(0.020)	(0.021)
Satisfied with democracy		−0.010	−0.010*		−0.007	−0.003
		(0.002)	(0.001)		(0.054)	(0.055)
Supports free market		−0.032	−0.035		0.050	0.049
		(0.029)	(0.025)		(0.031)	(0.027)
Supports capitalism		−0.039	−0.040		0.031	0.030
		(0.012)	(0.013)		(0.019)	(0.018)
Supports public sector		0.028	0.030		0.016	0.019
		(0.022)	(0.020)		(0.035)	(0.034)
Supports privatization		0.005	0.007		0.010	0.010
		(0.017)	(0.018)		(0.013)	(0.012)
Worse now than 12 months ago			−0.013			−0.040
			(0.008)			(0.029)
Worse in 12 months			−0.048			−0.013
			(0.026)			(0.024)
Dissatisfied with president			0.059***			0.035*
			(0.000)			(0.015)
Observations	1100	1096	1096	1223	1204	1204
Adjusted R2	0.013	0.068	0.070	0.060	0.080	0.081

Notes: Dependent variable is protest. Sample includes only individuals who are aware of the IMF SAP and only countries with a recent IMF program. Linear probability models with survey weights, country-fixed effects, and country-clustered standard errors. Significance levels: * $p<.1$ ** $p<.05$ *** $p<.01$

82 *International Relations*

awareness of respondents through an additional selection equation using all respondents. To predict IMF SAP awareness, we measure whether respondents are politically interested and politically knowledgeable. Both variables strongly correlate with IMF SAP awareness but should not directly affect protest. Using this estimation approach, the second-stage results concerning protest are qualitatively similar (Table A26).

In addition, we probe the applicability of our theoretical mechanism to ethnic politics. To that end, we compare protest patterns by respondents from ethnically powerless groups to respondents from powerful groups in countries with different exposure to IMF SAPs. The results indicate a protest-inducing effect of being a member of an ethnically powerless group when the country was under an IMF program, but not otherwise (Table A27). We probe whether and how ethnicity and partisanship co-produce protest under IMF SAP exposure. We find that individuals from ethnically powerless groups are more likely to protest when they also support the political opposition but less likely when they support the government (Table A28).

Furthermore, we utilize an alternative definition of protest that also includes protest inclinations. This is substantively interesting given that individuals may face obstacles to realizing protest preferences in many countries, for example, due to government repression. Our results are virtually unaffected: When individuals believe the IMF SAP made them worse off, they are more likely to consider protest. The percentage-point difference between partisans is at least 4.6 percent ($p < 0.05$) (Table A29).

Finally, we re-run our analyses with alternative econometric models. One alternative is to pool all observations and estimate probit models (Table A30). A more advanced alternative, which honors the nested nature of the data, is a multi-level random-intercept model, which assumes baseline country averages to be distributed normally around the mean (Table A31). In both cases, we find a strongly significant positive relationship between negative pocketbook evaluations and increased protest.

5.3 Survey Research on Asia

We now draw on the Asian Barometer to examine how perceptions of government biasedness – because of partisan-based distributive politics – affect protest. The unique setup of this survey also allows us to test if frustration with the IMF affects protest. Our sample includes only recent IMF program countries, as well as only respondents who have heard about the IMF program.

The dependent variable is PROTEST, a binary variable indicating whether respondents participated in protest over the past year. We first test whether

IMF Lending: Partisanship, Punishment, and Protest

protest is systematically related to if respondents believe their government is biased and whether they have a bad impression of the IMF. These two variables are proximate drivers. Our ultimate predictors include the partisan allegiance of the respondent, as well as the average number of binding conditions over the past three years.

Control variables are chosen to maximize overlap with our control set in the Afrobarometer sample. After running a barebones model with (only) country-fixed effects, we include standard demographics (male, age, urban, employed, years of education, support for democracy, support for the market economy) and subsequently relevant attitudes (confidence in the government, economic situation worse now than before, importance to obey government, and support for majority rule). The appendix to this section presents variable definitions and summary statistics. We estimate linear probability models with country-clustered standard errors.

5.3.1 Illustrative Evidence

We first conduct a subsample analysis, comparing the prevalence of protest among respondents who perceive their government as biased and those respondents who do not. As would be expected, the prevalence of protest is higher – twice as high – for the former respondents relative to the latter respondents (Figure A12), and highly statistically significant (p<0.001). Furthermore, we find that protest is more likely among individuals who have a bad impression of the IMF compared to those with a good impression. The difference is statistically significant but less pronounced than for government biasedness (Figure A13)

Figure 28 helps us to link protest to the underlying markers of distributive politics – the partisan allegiance of respondents – while also considering the context of IMF SAPs. It shows that when a country is not under an IMF program, there is a significant difference in the probability of protest between opposition supporters and government supporters (of about 2.8 percentage points). However, when a country undergoes an IMF SAP, the absolute difference in protest probabilities across different partisans increases (to about 3.6 percentage points). These patterns are consistent with our argument about the intensification of partisan conflict under IMF SAPs.

Figure 29 probes these patterns further by examining protest across different partisans and for different burdens of adjustment in IMF SAPs. We find that the partisan-based difference in protest is substantively sizable and strongly statistically significant in the high-conditionality scenario. About 12.0 percent (95% CI: 8.3–15.8%) of opposition supporters and 4.6 percent (95% CI: 2.9–6.4%) of

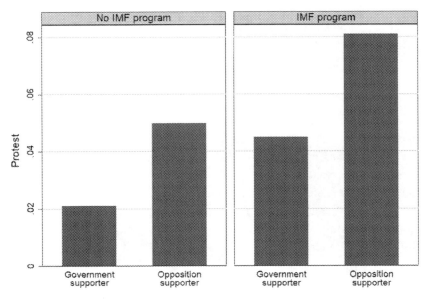

Figure 28 Partisan allegiance, IMF program exposure, and protest in Asia

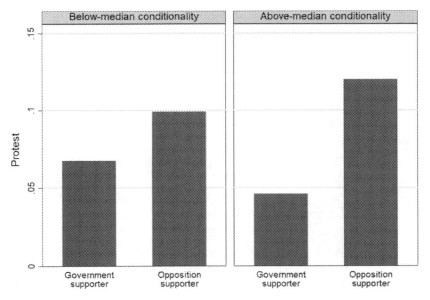

Figure 29 Partisan allegiance, IMF conditionality, and protest in Asian program countries

IMF Lending: Partisanship, Punishment, and Protest 85

government supporters protest under a high-conditionality scenario. In contrast, the partisan difference is smaller in the low-conditionality scenario, with 9.9 percent of opposition supporters (95% CI: 7.4–12.4%) and 6.7 percent of government supporters (95% CI: 2.9–10.6%) participating in protest respectively.

5.3.2 Regression Results

Table 13 shows the relationship between government biasedness, IMF program exposure, and protest in Asia. Two findings stand out. First, perceptions of government biasedness are related to significantly higher probabilities for protest. Second, where a government is under IMF program exposure, the effect of perceiving the government as biased on protest is higher compared to when a government is not under IMF exposure. In substantive terms, the average baseline probability of protest among individuals who perceive the government is biased is 3.8 percent (95% CI: 3.0–4.6%), which increases to 6.5 percent (95% CI: 4.0–8.9%) under an IMF program. These findings seem to suggest that IMF program exposure – which we know increases government biasedness on its own – amplifies protest proclivities among those who believe their government is biased.

Table 14 analyzes the relationship between government biasedness, IMF conditionality, and protest in Asian program countries. We find that as the number of IMF conditions increases, the protest-inducing effect of government biasedness increases. At the mean of IMF conditionality, the likelihood of protest is 5.5 percent (95% CI: 4.1–6.9%) for those who consider the government biased and 4.1 percent (95% CI: 3.2–4.9%) for those who do not. In the appendix, we plot the marginal effect of being an opposition supporter across the range of IMF conditions. Under a low-conditionality scenario, partisanship has no relationship with protest. Under a high-conditionality scenario, being an opposition supporter is related to an increased protest probability of two percentage points (p<0.05) (Figure A14).

Table 15 shows the relationship between partisan allegiances, IMF program participation, and protest. Opposition supporters are significantly more likely to protest when their country is under an IMF program. In contrast, the link between being an opposition supporter and protesting is not robust when a country is not under an IMF program. Substantively, this difference in opposition-driven protest amounts to about 5.4 percentage points (p<0.05). This finding supports the notion that IMF SAPs can amplify pre-existing partisan differences in protest inclination.

Table 16 relates protest to partisanship and IMF conditionality. Our conclusion is similar: as conditionality increases, the protest-inducing effect of being

Table 13 Government biasedness, IMF program exposure, and protest in Asian program countries

	(1)		(2)		(3)	
IMF exposure	−0.048***	(0.002)	−0.036**	(0.014)	−0.034**	(0.013)
Government is biased	0.013***	(0.003)	0.011***	(0.003)	0.010**	(0.003)
(Interaction)	0.027*	(0.011)	0.026*	(0.012)	0.026*	(0.012)
Male			0.014**	(0.005)	0.015**	(0.005)
(Logged) age			−0.011	(0.006)	−0.011	(0.006)
Urban			−0.009	(0.011)	−0.008	(0.012)
Employed			0.002	(0.008)	0.002	(0.008)
Education			−0.008	(0.005)	−0.008	(0.005)
Supports democracy			0.005	(0.004)	0.005	(0.005)
Democracy over growth			0.009	(0.005)	0.009	(0.005)
Economy got worse					0.007	(0.005)
Must obey government					−0.000	(0.007)
Supports majority rule					−0.001	(0.004)
Observations	13625		10912		10912	
Adjusted R2	0.019		0.028		0.028	

Notes: Dependent variable is protest. Linear probability model with survey weights, country-fixed effects, and country-clustered standard errors. Significance levels: * p<.1 ** p<.05 *** p<.01

Table 14 Government biasedness, IMF conditionality, and protest in Asian program countries

	(1)		**(2)**		**(3)**	
Average conditionality	0.005***	(0.000)	0.005***	(0.000)	0.005**	(0.001)
Government is biased	−0.001	(0.001)	−0.006*	(0.002)	−0.010*	(0.003)
(Interaction)	0.004***	(0.000)	0.004***	(0.000)	0.004***	(0.000)
Male			0.022	(0.012)	0.022	(0.012)
(Logged) age			−0.020	(0.011)	−0.020	(0.011)
Urban			−0.024	(0.012)	−0.023	(0.012)
Employed			−0.004	(0.011)	−0.004	(0.011)
Education			−0.013	(0.010)	−0.012	(0.010)
Supports democracy			0.015*	(0.004)	0.016*	(0.004)
Democracy over growth			0.015	(0.008)	0.015	(0.007)
Economy got worse					0.005	(0.002)
Must obey government					−0.012	(0.009)
Supports majority rule					−0.003	(0.007)
Observations	4002		4000		4000	
Adjusted R2	0.021		0.035		0.035	

Notes: Dependent variable is protest. Sample includes only countries with an IMF program. Linear probability model with survey weights, country-fixed effects, and country-clustered standard errors. Significance levels: * p<.1 ** p<.05 *** p<.01

Table 15 Partisan allegiances, IMF program exposure, and protest in Asia

	(1)		(2)		(3)	
IMF exposure	0.013	(0.012)	0.045	(0.023)	0.043	(0.029)
Opposition supporter	0.021**	(0.006)	0.015	(0.008)	0.015	(0.008)
(Interaction)	0.057***	(0.011)	0.054***	(0.010)	0.054***	(0.010)
Male			0.018**	(0.005)	0.018**	(0.005)
(Logged) age			−0.018	(0.015)	−0.017	(0.015)
Urban			−0.016	(0.016)	−0.016	(0.016)
Employed			−0.001	(0.009)	−0.001	(0.009)
Education			−0.009	(0.006)	−0.009	(0.005)
Supports democracy			0.002	(0.004)	0.002	(0.005)
Democracy over growth			0.008	(0.006)	0.008	(0.006)
Economy got worse					0.006	(0.008)
Must obey government					−0.004	(0.009)
Supports majority rule					0.002	(0.006)
Observations	8120		6706		6706	
Adjusted R2	0.022		0.031		0.031	

Notes: Dependent variable is protest. Linear probability model with survey weights, country-fixed effects, and country-clustered standard errors. Significance levels: * p<.1 ** p<.05 *** p<.01

Table 16 Partisan allegiances, IMF conditionality, and protest in Asian program countries

	(1)		(2)		(3)	
Average conditionality	−0.004***	(0.000)	−0.010	(0.002)	−0.010	(0.002)
Opposition supporter	−0.141***	(0.000)	−0.131**	(0.004)	−0.129**	(0.005)
(Interaction)	0.017***	(0.000)	0.015**	(0.000)	0.014**	(0.001)
Male			0.031	(0.008)	0.031	(0.008)
(Logged) age			−0.046	(0.018)	−0.046	(0.018)
Urban			−0.040	(0.008)	−0.038	(0.009)
Employed			−0.010	(0.005)	−0.010	(0.005)
Education			−0.018	(0.012)	−0.018	(0.011)
Supports democracy			0.011*	(0.001)	0.010*	(0.001)
Democracy over growth			0.019	(0.006)	0.018	(0.006)
Economy got worse					0.004	(0.005)
Must obey government					−0.019	(0.006)
Supports majority rule					0.005	(0.010)
Observations	2319		2317		2317	
Adjusted R2	0.011		0.038		0.038	

Notes: Dependent variable is protest. Sample includes only countries with an IMF program. Linear probability model with survey weights, country-fixed effects, and country-clustered standard errors. Significance levels: * p<.1 ** p<.05 *** p<.01

90 *International Relations*

an opposition supporter increases. The effect is most precisely estimated without controls but remains marginally significant even when adding a host of controls including attitudes, values, and beliefs. In the appendix, we plot the marginal effect of being an opposition supporter on protest for different levels of IMF conditionality (Figure A15). Albeit less precisely estimated, the partisan-based difference in protest is almost seven percentage points ($p<0.1$) across both program design scenarios.

5.3.3 Robustness Tests and Further Analyses

In the appendix, we probe whether our results hold when considering selection bias at the individual level. To that end, we include a selection equation modeling whether individuals have heard about the IMF SAP. We again use political interest and political knowledge to predict respondent awareness of the IMF SAP. We find that the partisan difference concerning protest is higher in countries that undergo an IMF program (Table A32). Among IMF SAP countries, we find that opposition supporters are more likely to protest especially when programs entail more adjustment burdens (Table A33). Taken together, these results are in line with our argument about the implications of partisan-based politics in the implementation of IMF SAPs.

5.4 Survey Research on Latin America

The Latinobarometer sample allows us to test whether greater dissatisfaction with public services – induced by experience of structural adjustment – affects the prevalence of protest. We first use all countries to analyze whether exposure to IMF SAPs moderates this relationship, before comparing only countries with an IMF SAP exposure but a different number of IMF conditions. As in the Asian sample, an exposed country must have been under an IMF program in any year during the three years preceding the survey year.

The dependent variable is a binary variable capturing whether a respondent participated in one of three kinds of political behavior in the past twelve months: lawful demonstrations, unlawful demonstrations, and anti-government riots. We chose these three behaviors to match the description of protest in the other regional surveys as closely as possible.

Key predictors include (dis)satisfaction with the quality of public services and dissatisfaction with the functioning of the market economy as potential proximate drivers of protest. Because our ultimate interest is in the consequences of partisan politics under IMF programs, we consider two additional sets of variables. The first is the partisan allegiance measure of a respondent, which captures whether a respondent has a different ideology than the party that held office for the preponderance of the three years before the survey year. The second set includes the two country-level indicators capturing IMF program exposure and the average number of binding conditions, both measured over the three years prior to the survey.

Control variables are identical to our analyses on evaluations, given that protest will likely be driven by the same underlying structural forces that also drive the grievances that make people protest. Our three successive sets of controls, therefore, include country-fixed effects, standard demographics, attitudes, beliefs, and values. We conduct linear probability models with country-clustered standard errors.

5.4.1 Illustrative Evidence

Using simple bivariate analysis, we examine whether protest is more likely when people are more dissatisfied with the evolution of public services that are plausibly affected by IMF SAPs. Figure 30 does not yield a clear-cut picture. While protest is significantly higher among those who believe that the quality of public schools had worsened, protest is unaffected by different perceptions of how the quality of public hospitals had evolved. The figures are based only on countries that had IMF program exposure in the three years before the survey.

We also examine how partisan differences in protest evolve if a country undergoes an IMF program, especially if that program has many conditions. Figure 31 shows that among countries that had IMF exposure, the partisan difference in protest is significantly higher for high-conditionality programs, compared to low-conditionality programs ($p<0.01$).

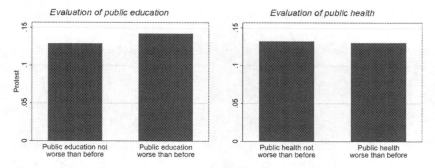

Figure 30 Evaluations of public services and protest in Latin American program countries

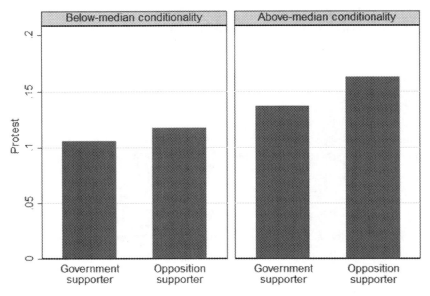

Figure 31 Partisan allegiances, IMF conditionality, and protest

5.4.2 Regession Results

We now turn to multivariate regression analysis for the above relationships. Table 17 examines the relationship between partisan allegiances, IMF program participation, and protest. We find that people who were aligned with the opposition are no more likely to protest than government supporters. This result holds regardless of whether a country was under an IMF program or not.

Table 18 shows the relationship between partisan allegiances, IMF conditionality, and protest in Latin American program countries. We find a significantly positive interaction effect between being an opposition supporter and the number of binding conditions in the program in two models. We consider the barebones model as less credible as it does not adjust for demographic differences. In sum, the results provide some evidence to suggest that governments lump the adjustment costs of more demanding IMF programs on opposition supporters, whose likelihood of protest increases as a result.

5.5 World Values Survey

Finally, we draw on the combined longitudinal WVS dataset covering respondents from six waves in 102 countries in the period from 1981 to 2019 (Inglehart et al. 2014). While the WVS dataset lacks a clean measure of partisan allegiance, it still allows us to probe the generalizability of our results across all world regions using the same measures. Furthermore, the greater country-year

Table 17 Partisan allegiances, IMF program exposure, and protest in Latin America

	(1)		(2)		(3)	
IMF exposure	−0.024*	(0.012)	−0.047***	(0.011)	−0.049***	(0.011)
Opposition supporter	−0.000	(0.022)	−0.013	(0.016)	−0.012	(0.015)
(Interaction)	0.023	(0.027)	0.013	(0.020)	0.012	(0.018)
(Logged) age			0.022**	(0.009)	0.019*	(0.010)
Male			0.023***	(0.007)	0.018*	(0.009)
Parental education			0.013**	(0.005)	0.011**	(0.005)
Education			0.023***	(0.004)	0.027***	(0.004)
Civil activism			0.081***	(0.012)	0.080***	(0.012)
Wealth index			−0.003*	(0.001)	−0.003*	(0.001)
Information index			0.004***	(0.001)	0.003***	(0.001)
Supports democracy					0.035***	(0.012)
Supports market economy					−0.028*	(0.014)
Dissatisfied with president					0.046***	(0.013)
Officials are corrupt					−0.018**	(0.006)
Observations	12570		9390		8269	
Adjusted R2	0.017		0.076		0.077	

Notes: Dependent variable is protest. Linear probability model with survey weights, country-fixed effects, and country-clustered standard errors. Significance levels: * p<.1 ** p<.05 *** p<.01

Table 18 Partisan allegiances, IMF conditionality, and protest in Latin American program countries

	(1)		(2)		(3)	
Average conditionality	−0.000	(0.000)	−0.002	(0.002)	0.000	(0.002)
Opposition supporter	−0.007	(0.016)	−0.034***	(0.008)	−0.023*	(0.012)
(Interaction)	0.001	(0.001)	0.001***	(0.000)	0.001*	(0.001)
(Logged) age			0.016	(0.011)	0.010	(0.013)
Male			0.026***	(0.008)	0.021**	(0.009)
Parental education			0.013**	(0.005)	0.009	(0.006)
Education			0.022***	(0.006)	0.027***	(0.006)
Civil activism			0.069***	(0.009)	0.066***	(0.009)
Wealth index			−0.002	(0.002)	−0.002	(0.002)
Information index			0.004***	(0.001)	0.004***	(0.001)
Supports democracy					0.030**	(0.013)
Supports market economy					−0.015	(0.015)
Dissatisfied with president					0.028**	(0.010)
Officials are corrupt					−0.015**	(0.007)
Observations	9710		7076		6240	
Adjusted R2	0.009		0.058		0.058	

Notes: Dependent variable is protest. Sample includes only countries with a recent IMF program. Linear probability model with survey weights, country-fixed effects, and country-clustered standard errors. Significance levels: * p<.1 ** p<.05 *** p<.01

coverage of the WVS dataset allows us to account for the role of financial crises as a macro-level confounder of IMF SAPs.

Our key outcome is PROTEST, which comes directly from a WVS survey question asking respondents whether they attended any peaceful (lawful) demonstrations during the twelve months before the survey date. This item has a more limited coverage than outcomes like experienced hardships. However, its advantage is to ask individuals to report on a behavioral outcome over a defined period. The item is simple, asking whether people protested or not, without giving the response option where individuals can indicate that they would protest if they had the chance.

Turning to our predictors, we use the same setup as in the WVS analysis on experienced hardships. At the macro-level, we measure the share of years in the three-year period before the survey year in which a country has suffered a financial crisis (Laeven and Valencia 2013). We also measure whether a country had IMF program exposure in any of the three years before the survey year (Kentikelenis, Stubbs, and King 2016). For robustness checks, we consider two-year lags of these macro-level indicators. At the micro-level, we use our partisan alignment measure that is constructed by comparing the ideological self-placement of the respondent and the political ideology of the government from the Database of Political Institutions (Scartascini, Cruz, and Keefer 2018). We identify opposition supporters based on a mismatch between these two ideological measures. Again, the measure cannot tell us if people actively supported the party with which they align but captures the potential for people to do so given their ideological alignment.

By including fixed-effects for countries and survey years, we already block the confounding effect of any macro-level variable. At the micro-level, we control for the usual set of demographic variables and values, beliefs, and preferences. Standard demographics are dummies for male, age, married, educated, under-employed, and political interest, as well as household size. For values, beliefs, and preferences, we measure demand for democracy, priority for growth, preference for equality, and confidence in government. The supplemental appendix presents variable definitions and descriptive statistics for all the variables (Table A5).

5.5.1 Illustrative Evidence

Figure 32 shows the partisan difference in protest for countries facing financial turmoil. Where countries attempted crisis resolution without the IMF, the partisan gap is 5.8 (95% CI: 2.3–9.4) percentage points, a relatively small difference. In contrast, with IMF involvement, the partisan gap is much higher, namely 20.5 (95% CI: 15.5–25.5) percentage points. We also observe lower

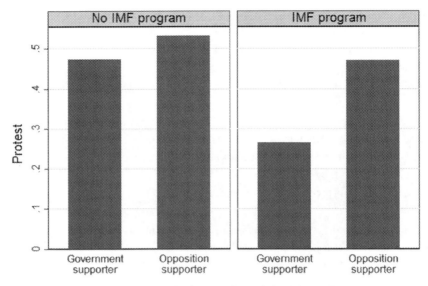

Figure 32 Partisan allegiances, financial crisis, and protest

absolute levels of protest for both partisans in the cases with IMF programs compared to crisis cases without IMF programs. However, it must be borne in mind that these results are correlational and should not be interpreted as evidence of a protest-dampening causal effect of IMF programs.[14]

5.5.2 Regression Analysis

Table 19 shows the relationship between partisan allegiances and protest in the context of financial crises, distinguishing cases of IMF programs and cases without IMF programs. We find a significantly positive interaction effect between the incidence of a financial crisis and being an opposition supporter on the likelihood of protest in the subsample of countries with IMF program participation. The partisan difference in protest is at least 9.6 (95% CI: 1.0–18.2) percentage points. This is a sizable effect, considering that only about 24.2 percent of the population actively engaged in protest in the entire sample. In contrast, where countries facing financial turmoil attempted to resolve their crises without IMF programs, we do not find a significant partisan gap concerning protest.

The results are stable across different sets of controls, and the estimates of the control variables are consistent with theoretical expectations. For example, we find that protest is more prevalent among males, the unmarried, fully employed

---

[14] For example, it could be that more authoritarian states receive IMF programs and thus protest is less likely to occur in these cases (Vreeland 2003).

Table 19 Partisan allegiances, financial crisis, and protest by IMF exposure

	Crisis resolution with IMF program						Crisis resolution without program					
	(1)		(2)		(3)		(4)		(5)		(6)	
Financial crisis	0.781***	(0.068)	0.845***	(0.080)	0.848***	(0.022)	0.018	(0.083)	−0.050	(0.171)	−0.101	(0.162)
Opposition supporter	0.022	(0.013)	0.016	(0.013)	0.015	(0.013)	0.009	(0.017)	0.004	(0.017)	0.000	(0.017)
(Interaction)	0.129***	(0.037)	0.099**	(0.040)	0.096**	(0.043)	0.021	(0.074)	0.030	(0.090)	0.029	(0.093)
Male			0.035***	(0.009)	0.034***	(0.010)			0.017***	(0.006)	0.014**	(0.005)
(Logged) age			−0.015	(0.015)	−0.020	(0.017)			−0.023	(0.018)	−0.026	(0.019)
Married			−0.023***	(0.006)	−0.028***	(0.008)			−0.008	(0.007)	−0.010	(0.007)
Household size			0.001	(0.003)	0.001	(0.003)			−0.004	(0.003)	−0.004	(0.003)
Underemployed			−0.040***	(0.009)	−0.039***	(0.010)			−0.011*	(0.006)	−0.011*	(0.006)
Educated			0.077***	(0.018)	0.069***	(0.020)			0.053***	(0.012)	0.052***	(0.013)
Politically interested			0.097***	(0.011)	0.098***	(0.012)			0.092***	(0.010)	0.098***	(0.011)
Demand for democracy					0.017	(0.012)					0.013	(0.011)
Priority for growth					−0.032***	(0.009)					−0.015*	(0.008)
Preference for equality					0.007	(0.011)					0.017*	(0.009)
Confidence in government					−0.037***	(0.013)					−0.025**	(0.010)
Observations	24180		21606		17017		36220		33609		29333	
Countries	28		28		28		44		43		43	
Adjusted R2	0.224		0.250		0.266		0.340		0.357		0.358	

Notes: Dependent variable is protest. Linear probability model with survey weights, country-fixed effects, year-fixed effects, and country-clustered standard errors. Significance levels: * p<.1 ** p<.05 *** p<.01

respondents (who have the most to lose from cuts), the educated, and the politically interested. We also find that respondents who prioritize economic growth and who have confidence in their government are less likely to protest. Our estimates are based on a moderate number of countries ($N \leq 44$) and survey waves ($N \leq 9$), and the overall model fit is sizable.

In the robustness checks, we probe an alternative operationalization of the key predictors using twice-lagged macro-predictors for financial crises and IMF programs. We find some evidence for a higher partisan gap with respect to protest when a crisis country underwent an IMF program. The partisan difference is only marginally significant in one model (Table A34). These patterns suggest that the timing of financial turmoil and IMF intervention is crucial when considering protest outcomes, as there seems to be a time lag between implementation of reforms, mobilization of protesters, and actual protest.

6 Discussion and Conclusion

How do governments implement policy demands of international financial institutions such as the IMF? We argued that governments use the discretion afforded to them in IMF programs to punish opposition supporters while protecting their own partisans. While distributive politics is commonplace, we expected that IMF programs amplify such distributive politics because they provide governments with opportunities to lump adjustment burdens upon opposition supporters. Our argument has three observable implications. First, we should find that individual experiences of IMF SAPs diverge depending on the partisan allegiances of citizens with their government. Second, we should find wider partisan gaps in relevant perceptions of individual wellbeing and satisfaction with public services when a country is under an IMF program, and especially if such program entails many conditions. Third, because of partisan-based distributive politics, we should find greater divergence in the probability of protest for opposition supporters relative to government supporters under an IMF program, especially when a program entails many conditions.

Using individual-level data from Afrobarometer (1999–2001), Asian Barometer (2005–8), Latinobarometer (2005), and the World Values Survey (1981–2019), as well as country-level data on IMF programs and IMF conditionality, we found evidence consistent with these expectations. In sub-Saharan Africa, opposition supporters are more likely to report that the IMF SAP made their life worse. Partisan differences in these pocketbook evaluations are particularly pronounced where a country is currently under an IMF program and when the IMF program entails an above-median number of IMF conditions.

These results withstand a battery of robustness tests, including controlling for general perceptions of the government and using objective hardships as an alternative outcome. We assess the generalizability of the results beyond Africa. In Asia, we find that opposition supporters are more likely than government supporters to think that the government is biased in its treatment of people. This partisan gap in assessments widens where a country has IMF program exposure, especially when IMF SAPs included an above-median number of IMF conditions. In Latin America, we found no clear evidence that opposition supporters are more dissatisfied than government supporters with the quality of public services when their countries were under IMF programs or when these programs had more conditions. In the WVS, we found widening partisan gaps in respondents reported income and deprivation when countries in financial turmoil turned to the IMF for crisis resolution. In contrast, we did not find significant partisan gaps when countries dealt with financial crises without IMF programs. These results suggest that it is not the financial troubles themselves, but the distinct choices that governments make in response to IMF policy demands that intensify partisan gaps.

Partisan bias in the implementation of IMF SAPs does not only affect attitudes but also drives protest. In sub-Saharan Africa, people who believe the IMF SAP made their lives worse are significantly more likely to protest. We also find that IMF program participation by the government provides a trigger for opposition supporters to mobilize, especially when IMF programs entail an above-median number of conditions. These findings again are robust to alternative explanations and estimation strategies. Mirroring our findings for Africa, we find in Asian countries where people perceive their government as biased, they are more likely to protest, especially under circumstances of IMF program exposure and extensive IMF conditionality. We also find that opposition supporters protest more than government supporters only when the country has had IMF exposure and when IMF programs included an above-mean number of policy conditions. In Latin America, the picture is more nuanced. Simply being under an IMF program does not make people aligned with the opposition more likely to protest compared to government supporters. But we find that a greater number of IMF conditions increases the likelihood of protest among opposition supporters. In the WVS, we found evidence of greater partisan gaps when countries in financial crises requested IMF programs, compared to when they had financial crises and did not undergo IMF programs. Taken together, a plausible interpretation of these findings is that governments allocate greater adjustment burdens onto opposition supporters when they face IMF programs with a higher number of policy conditions.

We note some limitations of our research. First and foremost, despite their potential to offer valuable insights into our research questions, the regional barometer and World Values surveys have not been designed to study the distributive politics of SAPs. The most important limitation is that they only provide a snapshot of individual experiences at specific time points. In an ideal scenario, we would have repeated observations for the same individuals to track changes in their attitudes, perceptions, and behaviors as IMF SAPs unfold. With only a cross-sectional dataset of individuals, we cannot control for unobserved respondent heterogeneity, which could drive our main outcomes of interest. We, therefore, preferred questions that include an implicit baseline for the same respondent, by asking them to compare their current life situation to their situation a year ago. However, not all barometers have worded the relevant questions in this way. Another limitation is that relevant questions are not always available in the surveys, and even if they are, they are worded differently so that direct comparisons are difficult. The most obvious example of this is the different ways in which partisan allegiances have been measured, with the Latinobarometer and WVS posing the greatest challenges for a valid test of our argument. We, therefore, caution against direct comparisons across barometers but instead emphasize opportunities for untangling causal mechanisms.

A final issue pertains to the external validity of our findings along the time dimension. Our surveys were taken at a time in which many countries were under IMF SAPs, sometimes with intrusive conditionality. On the one hand, this ensures that our results speak to the distributive politics under IMF SAPs at this critical point in time. The significance of these IMF SAPs in the recent history of many developing countries justifies our analysis of these surveys. A practical consideration was that subsequent surveys have not included questions on IMF SAPs, which limited our analysis to this time frame. On the other hand, there may be concerns that structural adjustment is no longer an issue, given that the IMF has reformed its lending programs and hence governments may have fewer opportunities to allocate adjustment burdens according to a partisan logic. We argue that our results are still relevant today because, despite changes in IMF rhetoric, its day-to-day practice of conditionality has not significantly changed (Kentikelenis, Stubbs, and King 2016). We would therefore contend that governments still have enlarged scope for distributive politics in the context of IMF programs. In addition, our analysis remains relevant because international financial institutions are now politicized more than ever before (Copelovitch and Pevehouse 2019; Walter 2021; Zürn 2018).

Avenues for future work include survey experiments designed to capture the partisan bias in the implementation of IMF SAPs. Researchers could also refine our study by further differentiating along the types of discretion examined in previous research. Finally, while our argument and analysis focused on IMF lending, we would expect to see more partisan-biased implementation of reforms under any external financier that uses intense conditionality in exchange for financial support. This could manifest itself in other scenarios including World Bank structural adjustment programs, as well as bilateral bailouts or aid packages including conditionality. We leave it to future researchers to probe the generalizability of the findings concerning different external creditors.

References

Abdulai, Abdul-Gafaru, and Sam Hickey. 2016. "The Politics of Development under Competitive Clientelism: Insights from Ghana's Education Sector." *African Affairs* 115(458): 44–72.

Abouharb, M. Rodwan, and David L. Cingranelli. 2007. *Human Rights and Structural Adjustment*. Cambridge: Cambridge University Press.

    2009. "IMF Programs and Human Rights, 1981–2003." *Review of International Organizations* 4: 47–72.

Akonor, Kwame. 2013. *Africa and IMF Conditionality: The Unevenness of Compliance, 1983–2000*. London: Routledge.

Almeida, Paul. 2019. *Social Movements: The Structure of Collective Mobilization*. Los Angeles: University of California Press.

Almeida, Paul, and Amalia Pérez-Martin. 2022. *Collective Resistance to Neoliberalism*. Cambridge: Cambridge University Press.

Almond, Gabriel A., and Sidney Verba. 1963. *An Approach to Political Culture*. Princeton: Princeton University Press.

Anaxagorou, Christiana, Georgios Efthyvoulou, and Vassilis Sarantides. 2020. "Electoral Motives and the Subnational Allocation of Foreign Aid in Sub-Saharan Africa." *European Economic Review* 127: article 103430. https://doi.org/10.1016/j.euroecorev.2020.103430.

Anebo, Felix K. G. 2001. "The Ghana 2000 Elections: Voter Choice and Electoral Decisions." *African Journal of Political Science/Revue Africaine de Science Politique* 6(1): 69–88.

Appiah-Kubi, Kojo. 2001. "State-Owned Enterprises and Privatisation in Ghana." *Journal of Modern African Studies* 39(2): 197–229.

Arce, Moises, and Jorge Mangonnet. 2013. "Competitiveness, Partisanship, and Subnational Protest in Argentina." *Comparative Political Studies* 46(8): 895–919.

Auvinen, Juha Y. 1996. "IMF Intervention and Political Protest in the Third World: A Conventional Wisdom Refined." *Third World Quarterly* 17(3): 377–400.

Azam, Jean-Paul. 2008. "The Political Geography of Redistribution." In *The Political Economy of Economic Growth in Africa 1960–2000*, ed. Benno Ndulu, Stephen A. O'Connell, Robert H. Bates, Paul Collier, and Chukwuma C. Soludo. Cambridge: Cambridge University Press, 225–48.

Babb, Sarah L. 2013. "The Washington Consensus as Transnational Policy Paradigm: Its Origins, Trajectory and Likely Successor." *Review of International Political Economy* 20(2): 268–97.

References

Barkan, Joel D. 2004. "Kenya after Moi." *Foreign Affairs* 83(1): 87–100.

Bas, Muhammet A., and Randall W. Stone. 2014. "Adverse Selection and Growth under IMF Programs." *Review of International Organizations* 9(1): 1–28.

Bates, Robert H. 1993. "'Urban Bias': A Fresh Look." *Journal of Development Studies* 29: 219–28.

Beazer, Quintin H., and Byungwon Woo. 2015. "IMF Conditionality, Government Partisanship, and the Progress of Economic Reforms." *American Journal of Political Science* 60(2): 304–21.

Beiser-McGrath, Janina, Carl Müller-Crepon, and Yannick I. Pengl. 2020. "Who Benefits? How Local Ethnic Demography Shapes Political Favoritism in Africa." *British Journal of Political Science* 51(4), 1582–600.

Bienen, Henry S., and Mark Gersovitz. 1985. "Economic Stabilization, Conditionality, and Political Stability." *International Organization* 39(4): 729–54.

Biglaiser, Glen, and Ronald J. McGauvran. 2022. "The Effects of IMF Loan Conditions on Poverty in the Developing World." *Journal of International Relations and Development* 25: 806–33.

Boafo-Arthur, Kwame. 1999. "Ghana: Structural Adjustment, Democratization, and the Politics of Continuity." *African Studies Review* 42(2): 41–72.

Bond, Patrick. 1998. "Privatisation, Participation and Protest in the Restructuring of Municipal Services." *Urban Forum* 9(1): 37–75.

Bond, Patrick, and Shauna Mottiar. 2013. "Movements, Protests and a Massacre in South Africa." *Journal of Contemporary African Studies* 31(2): 283–302.

Branch, Adam, and Zachariah Mampilly. 2015. *Africa Uprising: Popular Protest and Political Change*. London: Bloomsbury Publishing.

Bratton, Michael, and Nicholas van de Walle. 1997. *Democratic Experiments in Africa: Regime Transitions in Comparative Perspective*. Cambridge: Cambridge University Press.

Bratton, Michael, Ravi Bhavnani, and Tse-Hsin Chen. 2012. "Voting Intentions in Africa: Ethnic, Economic or Partisan?" *Commonwealth & Comparative Politics* 50(1): 27–52.

Brierley, Sarah. 2021. "Combining Patronage and Merit in Public Sector Recruitment." *Journal of Politics* 83(1): 182–97.

Briggs, Ryan C. 2012. "Electrifying the Base? Aid and Incumbent Advantage in Ghana." *The Journal of Modern African Studies* 50(4): 603–24.

2014. "Aiding and Abetting: Project Aid and Ethnic Politics in Kenya." *World Development* 64: 194–205.

Bueno de Mesquita, Bruce, and Alastair Smith. 2010. "Leader Survival, Revolutions, and the Nature of Government Finance." *American Journal of Political Science* 54(4): 936–50.

104 *References*

Bueno de Mesquita, Bruce, Alastair Smith, Randolph M. Siverson, and James D. Morrow. 2003. *The Logic of Political Survival*. Cambridge, MA: MIT Press.

Burgess, Robin, Remi Jedwab, Edward Miguel, Ameet Morjaria, and Gerard Padró I Miquel. 2015. "The Value of Democracy: Evidence from Road Building in Kenya." *American Economic Review* 105(6): 1817–51.

Campos, Jose Edgardo, and Hadi Salehi Esfahani. 1996. "Why and When Do Governments Initiate Public Enterprise Reform?" *World Bank Economic Review* 10(3): 451–85.

Caraway, Teri L., Stephanie J. Rickard, and Mark S. Anner. 2012. "International Negotiations and Domestic Politics: The Case of IMF Labor Market Conditionality." *International Organization* 66(1): 27–61. https://doi.org/10.1017/S0020818311000348.

Carlitz, Ruth D. 2017. "Money Flows, Water Trickles: Understanding Patterns of Decentralized Water Provision in Tanzania." *World Development* 93: 16–30.

Casper, Brett A. 2017. "IMF Programs and the Risk of a Coup d'état." *Journal of Conflict Resolution* 61(5): 964–96. https://doi.org/10.1177/00220027156 00759.

Casper, Brett A., and Scott A. Tyson. 2014. "Popular Protest and Elite Coordination in a Coup d'état." *Journal of Politics* 76(2): 548–64.

Chandra, Kanchan. 2007. *Why Ethnic Parties Succeed: Patronage and Ethnic Head Counts in India*. Cambridge: Cambridge University Press.

Chletsos, Michael, and Andreas Sintos. 2022a. "The Effects of IMF Conditional Programs on the Unemployment Rate." *European Journal of Political Economy* 76, article 102272.

 2022b. "The Effects of IMF Programs on Income Inequality: A Semi-Parametric Treatment Effects Approach." *International Journal of Development Issues* 21(2): 271–91.

CIS. 2005. "Kenya: Civil Society Angered by Arrests at World Trade Talks." March 4. *Catholic Information Service for* Africa. https://allafrica.com/stories/200503040490.html.

Clarke, Kevin A. 2005. "The Phantom Menace: Omitted Variable Bias in Econometric Research." *Conflict Management and Peace Science* 22(4): 341–52.

Collins, Charles David. 1988. "Local Government and Urban Protest in Colombia." *Public Administration and Development* 8(4): 421–36.

Copelovitch, Mark S. 2010. "Master or Servant? Common Agency and the Political Economy of IMF Lending." *International Studies Quarterly* 54(1): 49–77.

References

Copelovitch, Mark, and Jon C. W. Pevehouse. 2019. "International Organizations in a New Era of Populist Nationalism." *Review of International Organizations* 14(2): 169–86.

Crawford, Gordon, and Abdul-Gafaru Abdulai. 2009. "The World Bank and Ghana's Poverty Reduction Strategies: Strengthening the State or Consolidating Neoliberalism?" *Labour, Capital and Society/Travail, capital, et societe* 42(1/2): 82–115.

Daily Nation. 2000. "Kenya: Retirees Issue Ultimatum On Pay." *The Nation* (Nairobi). November 27. https://allafrica.com/stories/200011270924.html.

Dreher, Axel. 2006. "IMF and Economic Growth: The Effects of Programs, Loans, and Compliance with Conditionality." *World Development* 34(5): 769–88.

Dreher, Axel, and Martin Gassebner. 2012. "Do IMF and World Bank Programs Induce Government Crises? An Empirical Analysis." *International Organization* 66(2): 329–58. https://doi.org/10.1017/S0020818312000094

Dreher, Axel, and Stefanie Walter. 2010. "Does the IMF Help or Hurt? The Effect of IMF Programs on the Likelihood and Outcome of Currency Crises." *World Development* 38(1): 1–18.

Dreher, Axel, Andreas Fuchs, Bradley Parks, Austin Strange, and Michael J. Tierney. 2022. *Banking on Beijing: The Aims and Impacts of China's Overseas Development Program*. Cambridge: Cambridge University Press.

Dreher, Axel, Andreas Fuchs, Roland Hodler, et al. 2019. "African Leaders and the Geography of China's Foreign Assistance." *Journal of Development Economics* 140(April): 44–71.

Duch, Raymond M., and Randy Stevenson. 2006. "Assessing the Magnitude of the Economic Vote over Time and across Nations." *Electoral Studies* 25 (3): 528–47.

Easterly, William. 2005. "What Did Structural Adjustment Adjust? The Association of Policies and Growth with Repeated IMF and World Bank Adjustment Loans." *Journal of Development Economics* 76(1): 1–22.

Ejdemyr, Simon, Eric Kramon, and Amanda Lea Robinson. 2018. "Segregation, Ethnic Favoritism, and the Strategic Targeting of Local Public Goods." *Comparative Political Studies* 51(9): 1111–43.

Ellis-Jones, Mark. 2002. "States of Unrest II: Resistance to IMF and World Bank Policies in Poor Countries." www.globaljustice.org.uk/wp-content/uploads/2015/02/states_of_unrest_ii.pdf.

Ellis, Stephen, and Ineke Van Kessel. 2008. "Introduction: African Social Movements Or Social Movements In Africa?" In *Movers and Shakers: Social Movements in Africa*, ed. Stephen Ellis and Ineke Van Kessel. Leiden: Brill, 1–16.

106 *References*

Fernández-I-Marín, Xavier, Christoph Knill, and Yves Steinebach. 2021. "Studying Policy Design Quality in Comparative Perspective." *American Political Science Review* 115(3): 931–47.

Forster, Timon, Alexander E. Kentikelenis, Bernhard Reinsberg, Thomas H. Stubbs, and Lawrence P. King. 2019. "How Structural Adjustment Programs Affect Inequality: A Disaggregated Analysis of IMF Conditionality, 1980–2014." *Social Science Research* 80: 83–113.

Garuda, Gopal. 2000. "The Distributional Effects of IMF Programs: A Cross-Country Analysis." *World Development* 28(6): 1031–51.

Gayi, Samuel K. 1991. "Adjustment and 'Safety-Netting': Ghana's Programme of Actions to Mitigate the Social Costs of Adjustment (PAMSCAD)." *Journal of International Development* 3(4): 557–64.

Gehring, Kai, and Valentin F. Lang. 2020. "Stigma or Cushion? IMF Programs and Sovereign Creditworthiness." *Journal of Development Economics* 146: article 102507. https://doi.org/10.1016/j.jdeveco.2020.102507.

GhanaWeb. 1999a. "NDC Expresses Concern over Sale of Gold Reserves by IMF and UK." www.ghanaweb.com/GhanaHomePage/NewsArchive/artikel.php?ID=7914.

1999b. "S. Africa Says European Gold Tour Cancelled." www.ghanaweb.com/GhanaHomePage/business/S-Africa-says-European-gold-tour-cancelled-7729.

2000. "IMF Criticises Ghana Wage, Tax Increases." May 31. https://mobile.ghanaweb.com/GhanaHomePage/NewsArchive/IMF-criticises-Ghana-wage-tax-increases-10430.

2001a. "Budget Is a Foundation Budget – Nduom." April 4. www.ghanaweb.com/GhanaHomePage/NewsArchive/2001-Budget-is-a.

2001b. "IMF, World Bank Support Ghana." July 3. www.ghanaweb.com/GhanaHomePage/NewsArchive/IMF-World-Bank-support-Ghana-16322.

2001c. "Kufuor's Arrival Means Big Changes for Ghana Business." January 11 www.ghanaweb.com/GhanaHomePage/business/Kufuor-s-arrival-means-big-.

Githahu, Mwangi, and Beauttah Omanga. 2003. "Kenya: Ominous Turn in Pay Rise Hopes for Civil Servants." https://allafrica.com/stories/200312080181.html.

Grossman, Gene M., and Elhanan Helpman. 1994. "Protection for Sale." *American Economic Review* 84(4): 833–50.

Gurr, Ted R. 1969. "A Comparative Study of Civil Strife." In *Violence in America: Historical and Comparative Perspectives*, ed. Hughes D. Graham and Ted R. Gurr. Washington, DC: The White House, 443–86.

References

Greene, William H. 2003. *Econometric Analysis*, 4th ed. London: Pearson Education.

Haggard, Stephan, and Robert R. Kaufman. 1992. *The Politics of Economic Adjustment: International Constraints, Distributive Conflicts, and the State*. Princeton: Princeton University Press.

Haggard, Stephan, and Steven B. Webb. 1993. "What Do We Know about the Political Economy of Economic Policy Reform?" *World Bank Research Observer* 8(2): 143–68.

Handley, Antoinette. 2007. "Business, Government, and the Privatisation of the Ashanti Goldfields Company in Ghana." *Canadian Journal of African Studies/La Revue canadienne des études africaines* 41(1): 1–37.

Harding, Robin. 2015. "Attribution and Accountability: Voting for Roads in Ghana." *World Politics* 67(4): 656–89.

Harris, Adam S., and Erin Hern. 2019. "Taking to the Streets: Protest as an Expression of Political Preference in Africa." *Comparative Political Studies* 52(8): 1169–99.

Harris, J. Andrew, and Daniel N. Posner. 2019. "(Under What Conditions) Do Politicians Reward Their Supporters? Evidence from Kenya's Constituencies Development Fund." *American Political Science Review* 113(1): 123–39.

Harsch, Ernest. 2009. "Urban Protest in Burkina Faso." *African Affairs* 108 (431): 263–88.

Hartzell, Caroline A., Matthew Hoddie, and Molly Bauer. 2010. "Economic Liberalization via IMF Structural Adjustment: Sowing the Seeds of Civil War?" *International Organization* 64(2): 339–56.

Herbst, Jeffrey. 1990. "The Structural Adjustment of Politics in Africa." *World Development* 18(7): 949–58.

IMF. 1996. "Kenya – Enhanced Structural Adjustment Facility – Policy Framework Paper for 1996–1998." Washington, DC: IMF. www.imf.org/external/np/pfp/kenya/kenya.pdf.

1998. *Minutes of the Executive Board Meeting 98/122*. Washington, DC: IMF: https://archivescatalog.imf.org/search/simple.

1999. *IMF Approves ESAF Loan for Ghana*. Washington, DC: IMF. www .imf.org/en/News/Articles/2015/09/14/01/49/pr9916.

2000. "Memorandum of Economic and Financial Policies of the Government of Ghana for 2000." www.imf.org/external/np/loi/2000/gha/01/index.htm.

2001a. *Conditionality in Fund-Supported Programs*. Washington, DC: IMF.

2001b. *Structural Conditionality in Fund-Supported Programs*. Washington, DC: IMF.

References

Inglehart, R., C. Haerpfer, A. Moreno, et al. 2014. "World Values Survey: All Rounds: Country-Pooled Datafile 1981–2014." Madrid: JD Systems Institute. www.worldvaluessurvey.org/WVSDocumentationWV (July 17, 2020).

Isaksson, Ann Sofie, and Andreas Kotsadam. 2018. "Chinese Aid and Local Corruption." *Journal of Public Economics* 159: 146–59.

Ito, Takatoshi. 2012. "Can Asia Overcome the IMF Stigma?" *American Economic Review* 102(3): 198–202.

Jablonski, Ryan S. 2014. "How Aid Targets Votes: The Impact of Electoral Incentives on Foreign Aid Distribution." *World Politics* 66(2): 293–330.

Jeong, Ho-Won. 1995. "Liberal Economic Reform in Ghana: A Contested Political Agenda." *Africa Today* 42(4): 82–104.

Johnson, Omotunde, and Joanne Salop. 1980. "Stabilization Programs and Income Distribution." *Finance & Development* 17(4): 28–40.

Kamau, John. 2000. "Kenya: Civil Servants Face Job Loss Due to IMF Policies." Gemini News Service. October 6. www.corpwatch.org/article/kenya-civil-servants-face-job-loss-due-imf-policies.

2003. "Kenya: Guarded Praise From IMF." *East African Standard*. October 26. https://allafrica.com/stories/200310270241.html.

Kaufman, Robert R., and Leo Zuckermann. 1998. "Attitudes toward Economic Reform in Mexico: The Role of Political Orientations." *American Political Science Review* 92(2): 359–75.

Keen, David. 2005. "Liberalization and Conflict." *International Political Science Review* 26(1): 73–89.

Kentikelenis, Alexander E., and Sarah Babb. 2019. "The Making of Neoliberal Globalization: Norm Substitution and the Politics of Clandestine Institutional Change." *American Journal of Sociology* 124(6): 1720–62. www.journals.uchicago.edu/doi/10.1086/702900.

Kentikelenis, Alexander E., Thomas H. Stubbs, and Lawrence P. King. 2016. "IMF Conditionality and Development Policy Space, 1985–2014." *Review of International Political Economy* 23(4): 543–82.

Kisero, Jaindi. 2003. "Kenya: No Change With These Civil Servants." *The Nation* (Nairobi). December 10. https://allafrica.com/stories/200312100098.html.

Kithi, Ngumbao. 2000. "Kenya: Dismissals Improper, Says Kiliku." https://allafrica.com/stories/200009010429.html.

Kitschelt, Herbert, and Steven I. Wilkinson. 2007. *Patrons, Clients and Policies: Patterns of Democratic Accountability and Political Competition.* Cambridge: Cambridge University Press.

References

Kopecký, Petr. 2011. "Political Competition and Party Patronage: Public Appointments in Ghana and South Africa." *Political Studies* 59(3): 713–32.

Kopecký, Petr, Peter Mair, and Maria Spirova. 2012. *Party Patronage and Party Government in European Democracies*. Oxford: Oxford University Press.

Kopecký, Petr, Jan-Hinrik Meyer Sahling, Francisco Panizza et al. 2016. "Party Patronage in Contemporary Democracies: Results from an Expert Survey in 22 Countries from Five Regions." *European Journal of Political Research* 55(2): 416–31.

Kramon, Eric, and Daniel N. Posner. 2013. "Who Benefits from Distributive Politics? How the Outcome One Studies Affects the Answer One Gets." *Perspectives on Politics* 11(2): 461–74.

Laeven, Luc, and Fabian Valencia. 2013. "Systemic Banking Crises Database." *IMF Economic Review* 61(2): 225–70.

Lang, Valentin F. 2021. "The Economics of the Democratic Deficit: The Effect of IMF Programs on Inequality." *Review of International Organizations* 16(3): 599–623.

Lavine, Howard G., Christopher D. Johnston, and Marco R. Steenbergen. 2012. *The Ambivalent Partisan: How Critical Loyalty Promotes Democracy*. Oxford: Oxford University Press.

Lio Rosvold, E. 2020. "Disaggregated Determinants of Aid: Development Aid Projects in the Philippines." *Development Policy Review* 38(6): 783–803.

Lipscy, Phillip Y., and Haillie Na-Kyung Lee. 2019. "The IMF as a Biased Global Insurance Mechanism: Asymmetrical Moral Hazard, Reserve Accumulation, and Financial Crises." *International Organization* 73(1): 35–64.

Magaloni, Beatriz, and Jeremy Wallace. 2008. "Citizen Loyalty, Mass Protest and Authoritarian Survival." Paper presented at *Dictatorships: Their Governance and Social Consequences*, Princeton University.

Makoloo, Maurice O. 2005. *Kenya: Minorities, Indigenous Peoples and Ethnic Diversity*. London: Minority Rights Group International.

Marc, Alexandre, Carol Graham, Mark Schacter, and Mary Schmidt. 1995. *A Review of Design and Implementation in Sub-Saharan Africa*. Washington, DC: World Bank.

Mueller, Lisa. 2013. "Democratic Revolutionaries or Pocketbook Protesters? The Roots of the 2009–2010 Uprisings in Niger." *African Affairs* 112 (448): 398–420.

Mwenda, Andrew M., and Roger Tangri. 2005. "Patronage Politics, Donor Reforms, and Regime Consolidation in Uganda." *African Affairs* 104 (416): 449–67.

110 *References*

Nelson, Joan M. 1984. *The Politics of Stabilization: Adjustment Crisis in the Third World*. New Brunswick: Transaction Books.

——— 1992. "Poverty, Equity, and the Politics of Adjustment." In *The Politics of Economic Adjustment*, ed. Stephan Haggard and Robert R. Kaufman. Princeton: Princeton University Press, 222–69.

Ninsin, Kwame Akon. 1998. *Ghana: Transition to Democracy*. Dakar: CODESRIA.

Nooruddin, Irfan, and Joel W. Simmons. 2006. "The Politics of Hard Choices: IMF Programs and Government Spending." *International Organization* 60 (4): 1001–33.

Oberdabernig, Doris A. 2013. "Revisiting the Effects of IMF Programs on Poverty and Inequality." *World Development* 46: 113–42.

Ochieng, William Robert. 2002. *Historical Studies and Social Change in Western Kenya: Essays in Memory of Professor Gideon S. Were*. Nairobi: East African Publishers.

Oliveros, Virginia. 2021. *Patronage at Work: Public Jobs and Political Services in Argentina*. Cambridge: Cambridge University Press.

Olson, Mancur. 1971. *The Logic of Collective Action: Public Goods and the Theory of Groups*. Cambridge, MA: Harvard University Press.

Opiyo, Gordon. 2003a. "Kenya: Tough Demands Donors Want Kenya to Meet." https://allafrica.com/stories/200310270268.html.

——— 2003b. "Kenya: Winners and Losers in Changing Donor Tides." https://allafrica.com/stories/200311100314.html.

Ortiz, David G., and Sergio Béjar. 2013. "Participation in IMF-Sponsored Economic Programs and Contentious Collective Action in Latin America, 1980–2007." *Conflict Management and Peace Science* 30(5): 492–515.

Otieno, Isaiah Oduor. 2009. "Effects of the Civil Service Retrenchment Programme on Women in Nakuru Town." Master's thesis, Kenyatta University.

Panizza, Francisco, B. Guy Peters, and Conrado R. Ramos Larraburu. 2019. "Roles, Trust and Skills: A Typology of Patronage Appointments." *Public Administration* 97(1): 147–61.

Pastor, Manuel. 1987. "The Effects of IMF Programs in the Third World: Debate and Evidence from Latin America." *World Development* 15(2): 249–62.

——— 1988. *The International Monetary Fund And Latin America: Economic Stabilization And Class Conflict*. London: Routledge.

Payer, Cheryl. 1974. *The Debt Trap: The International Monetary Fund and the Third World*. New York: NYU Press.

References

PeaceFMOnline. 1996a. "Election 1996 Ashanti Region." https://ghanaelec
tions.peacefmonline.com/pages/1996/ashanti/.

  1996b. "Election 1996 Central Region." https://ghanaelections.peacefmon
line.com/pages/1996/central/.

Pilati, Katia. 2011. "Political Context, Organizational Engagement, and Protest
in African Countries." *Mobilization* 16(3): 351–68.

Pion-Berlin, David. 1983. "Political Repression and Economic Doctrines: The
Case of Argentina." *Comparative Political Studies* 16(1): 37–66.

Polak, Jacques J. 1991. "The Changing Nature of IMF Conditionality."
Washington, DC: IMF.

Poulton, Colin, and Karuti Kanyinga. 2014. "The Politics of Revitalising
Agriculture in Kenya." *Development Policy Review* 32(s2): s151–s172.

Rakodi, Carole, Rose Gatabaki-Kamau, and Nick Devas. 2000. "Poverty and
Political Conflict in Mombasa." *Environment and Urbanization* 12(1):
153–70.

Reddy, Sanjay. 1998. *Social Funds in Developing Countries: Recent
Experiences and Lessons*. New York: Unicef.

Reinsberg, Bernhard, and M. Rodwan Abouharb. 2022. "Partisanship, Protection,
and Punishment: How Governments Affect the Distributional Consequences
of International Monetary Fund Programs." *Review of International Political
Economy*. http://doi.org/10.1080/09692290.2022.2126513.

Reinsberg, Bernhard, Alexander Kentikelenis, and Thomas Stubbs. 2019.
"Creating Crony Capitalism: Neoliberal Globalization and the Fueling of
Corruption." *Socio-economic Review*. http://doi.org/10.1093/ser/mwz039.

Reinsberg, Bernhard, Andreas Kern, and Matthias Rau-Göhring. 2021. "The
Political Economy of IMF Conditionality and Central Bank
Independence." *European Journal of Political Economy* 68: article
101987.

Reinsberg, Bernhard, Thomas Stubbs, and Alexander Kentikelenis. 2021.
"Compliance, Defiance, and the Dependency Trap: International
Monetary Fund Program Interruptions and Their Impact on Capital
Markets." *Regulation & Governance* 16(4): 1022–41. http://doi.org/
10.1111/rego.12422.

  2022. "Unimplementable by Design? Understanding (Non-)Compliance with
International Monetary Fund Policy Conditionality." *Governance* 35(3):
689–715.

Reinsberg, Bernhard, Andreas Kern, Mirko Heinzel, and Saliha Metinsoy. 2023.
"Women's Leadership and the Gendered Consequences of Austerity in the
Public Sector: Evidence from IMF Programs." *Governance*: http://doi.org/
10.1111/gove.12764.

References

Reinsberg, Bernhard, Thomas Stubbs, Alexander Kentikelenis, and Lawrence King. 2019. "Bad Governance: How Privatization Increases Corruption in the Developing World." *Regulation and Governance* (May): 1–20.

Reno, William. 1996. "Ironies of Post-Cold War Structural Adjustment in Sierra Leone." *Review of African Political Economy* 23(67): 7–18.

Rickard, Stephanie J., and T. L. Caraway. 2019. "International Demands for Austerity: Examining the Impact of the IMF on the Public Sector." *Review of International Organizations* 14: 35–57.

Ritter, Emily H., and Courtenay R. Conrad. 2016. "Preventing and Responding to Dissent: The Observational Challenges of Explaining Strategic Repression." *American Political Science Review* 110(1): 85–99.

Robertson, Graeme B., and Emmanuel Teitelbaum. 2011. "Foreign Direct Investment, Regime Type, and Labor Protest in Developing Countries." *American Journal of Political Science* 55(3): 665–77.

Scartascini, Carlos, Cesi Cruz, and Philip Keefer. 2018. *The Database of Political Institutions 2017 (DPI2017)*. Washington, DC: Inter-American Development Bank. https://publications.iadb.org/en/database-political-institutions-2017-dpi2017.

Schmidt-Catran, Alexander W., and Malcolm Fairbrother. 2016. "The Random Effects in Multilevel Models: Getting Them Wrong and Getting Them Right." *European Sociological Review* 32(1): 23–38.

Shim, Sujeong. 2022. "Who Is Credible? Government Popularity and the Catalytic Effect of IMF Lending." *Comparative Political Studies* 55(13): 2147–77.

Sidell, Scott R. 1988. *International Monetary Fund and Third World Political Instability: Is There a Connection?* Cham: Springer.

Smith, Alastair, and James R. Vreeland. 2006. "The Survival of Political Leaders and IMF Programs: Testing the Scapegoat Hypothesis." In *Globalization and the Nation State: The Impact of the IMF and the World Bank*, ed. Stephen Kosack, Gustav Ranis, and James Vreeland. London: Routledge.

Stegmueller, Daniel. 2013. "How Many Countries for Multilevel Modeling? A Comparison of Frequentist and Bayesian Approaches." *American Journal of Political Science* 57(3): 748–61.

Stiglitz, Joseph E. 2002. *Globalization and Its Discontents*. New York: W. W. Norton & Company.

Stone, Randall W. 2002. *Lending Credibility: The International Monetary Fund and the Post-Communist Transition*. Princeton: Princeton University Press.

References 113

Stubbs, Thomas H., and Alexander Kentikelenis. 2018. "Targeted Social Safeguards in the Age of Universal Social Protection: The IMF and Health Systems of Low-Income Countries." *Critical Public Health* 28 (2): 132–39.

Stubbs, Thomas H., Alexnder E. Kentikelenis, Rebecca Ray, and Kevin P. Gallagher. 2022. "Poverty, Inequality, and the International Monetary Fund: How Austerity Hurts the Poor and Widens Inequality." *Journal of Globalization and Development* 13(1): 61–89.

Stubbs, Thomas H., Alexander Kentikelenis, David Stuckler, Martin McKee, and Lawrence King. 2017. "The Impact of IMF Conditionality on Government Health Expenditure: A Cross-National Analysis of 16 West African Nations." *Social Science and Medicine* 174(3): 220–27.

Stubbs, Thomas H., Bernhard Reinsberg, Alexander E. Kentikelenis, and Lawrence P. King. 2020a. "How to Evaluate the Effects of IMF Conditionality: An Extension of Quantitative Approaches and an Empirical Application to Government Education Expenditures." *Review of International Organizations* 15(1): 29–73.

2020b. "How to Evaluate the Effects of IMF Conditionality: An Extension of Quantitative Approaches and an Empirical Application to Public Education Spending." *Review of International Organizations* 15(1): 29–73.

Sunday Nation. 2000. "Kenya: Lay-Offs Flawed, Alleges Mokku." https://allafrica.com/stories/200012110137.html.

Szarzec, Katarzyna, Bartosz Totleben, and Dawid Pikatek. 2022. "How Do Politicians Capture a State? Evidence from State-Owned Enterprises." *East European Politics and Societies* 36(1): 141–72.

Tait, Alan A. 1989. *IMF Advice on Fiscal Policy.* Washington, DC: IMF.

Tarrow, Sidney. 1996. "Social Movements in Contentious Politics: A Review Article." *American Political Science Review* 90(4): 874–93.

The East African Standard. 2007. "Kenya: Parastatals, Making Profits?!" March 13. https://allafrica.com/stories/200703130446.html.

The Nation. 2009. "Kibaki Overturns Treasury Order on Development Spending." March 28. https://nation.africa/kenya/news/kibaki-overturns-treasury-order-ondevelopment.

2013. "Date with History: October 12, 1997." https://nation.africa/kenya/life-andstyle/.

2014. "Governors Ignore Minorities in Jobs." June 22. https://nation.africa/kenya/news/politics/governors-ignore-minorities-in-jobs-996772.

The New Humanitarian. 2000. "Government Increases Salaries by 20 per Cent." May 31. www.thenewhumanitarian.org/report/15391/ghana-government-increases-salaries-20-cent.

Theisen, Ole Magnus, Håvard Strand, and Gudrun Østby. 2020. "Ethno-Political Favouritism in Maternal Health Care Service Delivery: Micro-Level Evidence from Sub-Saharan Africa, 1981–2014." *International Area Studies Review* 23(1): 3–27.

Throup, David. 2003. "The Kenya General Election: December 27, 2002." *Africa Notes* 14. https://csis-website-prod.s3.amazonaws.com/s3fspublic/.

Tilly, Charles. 1978. *From Mobilization to Revolution*. London: Addison-Wesley.

Trasberg, Mart. 2021. "Informal Institutions, Protest and Public Goods Provision in Mexico." Tulane University, School of Liberal Arts.

Vogt, Manuel et al. 2015. "Integrating Data on Ethnicity, Geography, and Conflict: The Ethnic Power Relations Data Set Family." *Journal of Conflict Resolution* 59(7): 1327–42.

Vreeland, James R. 2002. "The Effect of IMF Programs on Labor." *World Development* 30(1): 121–39.

2003. *The IMF and Economic Development*. Cambridge: Cambridge University Press.

van de Walle, Nicolas. 2001. *African Economies and the Politics of Permanent Crisis, 1979–1999*. Cambridge: Cambridge University Press.

2007. "Meet the New Boss, Same as the Old Boss? The Evolution of Political Clientelism in Africa." In *Patrons, Clients and Policies: Patterns of Democratic Accountability and Political Competition*, ed. Herbert Kitschelt and Steven I. Wilkinson. Cambridge: Cambridge University Press.

Walter, Stefanie. 2013. *Financial Crises and the Politics of Macroeconomic Adjustments*. Cambridge: Cambridge University Press.

2021. "The Backlash Against Globalization." *Annual Review of Political Science* 24(1): 421–42.

Walton, John, and Charles Ragin. 1990. "Global and National Sources of Political Protest: Third World Responses to the Debt Crisis." *American Sociological Review* 55(6): 876–90.

Warf, Barney. 2017. "Geographies of African Corruption." *PSU Research Review* 1(1): 20–38. www.emeraldinsight.com/doi/10.1108/PRR-12-2016-0012.

Warigi, Gitau. 2000. "Kenya: Harsh Reality of Job Cuts Begins to Sink." https://allafrica.com/stories/200009030107.html.

Waterbury, John. 1992. "The Heart of the Matter? Public Enterprise and the Adjustment Process." In *The Politics of Economic Adjustment*, ed. Stephan Haggard and Robert R. Kaufman. Princeton: Princeton University Press, 182–220.

References

Woo, Byungwon. 2013. "Conditional on Conditionality: IMF Program Design and Foreign Direct Investment." *International Interactions* 39(3): 292–315.

Wrong, Michela. 2010. *It's Our Turn to Eat: The Story of a Kenyan Whistleblower*. London: Fourth Estate.

Youde, Jeremy. 2005. "Economics and Government Popularity in Ghana." *Electoral Studies* 24(1): 1–16.

Zack-Williams, Alfred B. 1999. "Sierra Leone: The Political Economy of Civil War, 1991–98." *Third World Quarterly* 20(1): 143–62.

Zárate, Rod. 2022. "Zárate's Political Collections." http://zarate.eu/.

Zürn, Michael. 2018. "Contested Global Governance." *Global Policy* 9(1): 138–45

Cambridge Elements ☰

International Relations

Series Editors

Jon C. W. Pevehouse
University of Wisconsin–Madison

Jon C. W. Pevehouse is Mary Herman Rubinstein Professor of Political Science and Public Policy at the University of Wisconsin–Madison. He has published numerous books and articles in IR in the fields of international political economy, international organizations, foreign policy analysis, and political methodology. He is a former editor of the leading IR field journal, International Organization.

Tanja A. Börzel
Freie Universität Berlin

Tanja A. Börzel is the Professor of political science and holds the Chair for European Integration at the Otto-Suhr-Institute for Political Science, Freie Universität Berlin. She holds a PhD from the European University Institute, Florence, Italy. She is coordinator of the Research College "The Transformative Power of Europe," as well as the FP7-Collaborative Project "Maximizing the Enlargement Capacity of the European Union" and the H2020 Collaborative Project "The EU and Eastern Partnership Countries: An Inside-Out Analysis and Strategic Assessment." She directs the Jean Monnet Center of Excellence "Europe and its Citizens."

Edward D. Mansfield
University of Pennsylvania

Edward D. Mansfield is the Hum Rosen Professor of Political Science, University of Pennsylvania. He has published well over 100 books and articles in the area of international political economy, international security, and international organizations. He is Director of the Christopher H. Browne Center for International Politics at the University of Pennsylvania and former program co-chair of the American Political Science Association.

Editorial Team

International Relations Theory

Jeffrey T. Checkel, European University Institute, Florence

International Security

Anna Leander, Graduate Institute Geneva

International Political Economy

Edward D. Mansfield, University of Pennsylvania

Stafanie Walter, University of Zurich

International Organisations

Tanja A. Börzel, Freie Universität Berlin

Jon C. W. Pevehouse, University of Wisconsin–Madison

About the Series

The Cambridge Elements Series in International Relations publishes original research on key topics in the field. The series includes manuscripts addressing international security, international political economy, international organizations, and international relations.

Cambridge Elements ☰

International Relations

Elements in the Series

Social Media and International Relations
Sarah Kreps

International Norms, Moral Psychology, and Neuroscience
Richard Price and Kathryn Sikkink

Across Type, Time and Space: American Grand Strategy in Comparative Perspective
Peter Dombrowski and Simon Reich

Contestations of the Liberal International Order
Fredrik Söderbaum, Kilian Spandler, Agnese Pacciardi

Domestic Interests, Democracy, and Foreign Policy Change
Brett Ashley Leeds, Michaela Mattes

Token Forces: How Tiny Troop Deployments Became Ubiquitous in UN Peacekeeping
Katharina P. Coleman, Xiaojun Li

The Dual Nature of Multilateral Development Banks
Laura Francesca Peitz

Peace in Digital International Relations
Oliver P. Richmond, Gëzim Visoka, Ioannis Tellidis

Regionalized Governance in the Global South
Brooke Coe, Kathryn Nash

Digital Globalization
Stephen Weymouth

After Hedging: Hard Choices for the Indo-Pacific States between the US and China
Kai He, Huiyun Feng

IMF Lending: Partisanship, Punishment, and Protest
Rodwan Abouharb, Bernhard Reinsberg

A full series listing is available at: www.cambridge.org/EIR

Printed in the United States
by Baker & Taylor Publisher Services